Nov 16, 1995

THE ZEN EYE

(2l

996 - 4296

Dosage   Etta

{ Looks better
out to dinner

THE ZEN EYE

A COLLECTION OF
ZEN TALKS BY SOKEI-AN

EDITED AND WITH AN INTRODUCTION BY
MARY FARKAS

WITH A FOREWORD BY
HUSTON SMITH

TOKYO   WEATHERHILL   NEW YORK

The Appendix is based on an article in *Zen Notes* XIII, no. 6,
June 1966, entitled "Zen Talks II" by Mary Farkas.

Second printing, 1994

Published by Weatherhill, Inc., 420 Madison Avenue, 15th Floor,
New York, NY 10017. Protected by copyright under terms of the
International Copyright Union; all rights reserved. Except for
fair use in book reviews, no part of this book may be reproduced
for any reason by any means, including any method of photographic
reproduction, without permission of the publisher. Printed in the
United States.

Library of Congress Cataloging in Publication Data

Sokei-an, 1882-1945
The Zen eye : a collection of talks / by Sokei-an ; edited
and with an introduiction by Mary Farkas.—1st ed.
p.   cm.
ISBN 0-8348-0272-4 (pbk.) : $12.95
1. Spiritual life—Zen Buddhism. 2. Zen Buddhism—Doctrines.
I. Farkas, Mary, 1910-1992. II. Title.
BQ9288.S65 1993
294.3'4—dc20   92-45803
                                                    CIP

TABLE OF CONTENTS

CONTENTS

FOREWORD

Some years ago my wife and I checked out a Native American restaurant in Vancouver that was rumored to serve tea, brewed from local leaves, that induced euphoria. Not in us, we concluded, as (cup after cup) we agreed that we were enjoying the meal but noticed no shift in consciousness. It was not until we were back in our hotel room that we realized we had had a smashingly marvelous evening.

Something analogous happened to me as I was reading these talks by Sokei-an. They started out seeming so down to earth that I had to remind myself that this was actually a book about religion. At some point, though—I couldn't say when, for the shift crept up on me—I realized that things looked different, including the subways and Central Park and gingko trees that Sokei-an had been talking about. They were bathed in something of the "shining trance" he tells us he entered in his early twenties and never left.

Though his lineage was somewhat outside the Japanese religious establishment, the way Sokei-an speaks of things as transparent to their infinite Source proves the authenticity, and indeed orthodoxy, of his Zen. For it is the distinguishing genius of Zen Buddhism (and its Chinese antecedent, Ch'an) to refuse to dislodge earth from heaven. That emphasis is (in its degree) unique within the historical religions, but it is the way tribal, pre-writing peoples see things regularly. Considered in this light, Ch'an and Zen are rivulets that perpetuate, in history, an early talent. Daily, in their monasteries, Zen monks recite the Heart Sutra's extended mantra:

> Form does not differ from emptiness;
>
> Emptiness does not differ from form.
>
> That which is form is emptiness;
>
> That which is emptiness, form.

A hair's-breadth's difference, and heaven and hell are set apart.

Zen Buddhists enact this central teaching by placing their palms together and bowing—joining their palms symbolizes the union of finite and infinite, while their bow evinces gratitude. Respecting this book, our gratitude goes to the loyal members of the First Zen Institute of America (the late Mary Farkas preeminent among them), whose devoted labors have brought it into being. Even more, though, our gratitude extends to the author of these talks, who left his home for a foreign land. Sokei-an kept such a low profile that his story is not widely known, so I shall summarize it.

This book is published on the centenary of the 1893 World Parliament of Religions in Chicago. That Parliament provided the platform on which Sokei-an's Dharma grandfather, Soen Shaku, introduced Zen (and in a larger sense Buddhism) to the West. Having done so, he directed his heir, Sokatsu Shaku, to continue his mission, and the latter, after laboring on the West Coast for a while, directed Daisetz Suzuki to translate Zen texts, and Sokei-an to found, in New York City, the First Zen Institute of America, which continues to this day.

A third student of Sokatsu Shaku, Zuigan Goto, remained in Kyoto and was the Roshi under whom I trained. This makes the author of this book my Dharma uncle, for he and my teacher were Dharma brothers in having the same teacher. It is for me, therefore, an honor of the highest grade to be accorded the privilege of saluting, through this Preface, one of the wisest teachers of our century—one who, until now, has not been widely recognized. It is his legacy that we hold in our hands.

Huston Smith

INTRODUCTION

Sokei-an Shigetsu Sasaki was the first Zen master to make his home in America and to dedicate his life to introducing the Zen of "sudden" awakening to Americans. When he began to give lectures at 63 West 70th Street in Manhattan in the 1930s, he had no way of knowing if his words would ever be remembered, much less appear in print. Bringing Zen to America, he said, was as uncertain as holding a lotus to a rock, hoping it will take root.

Sokei-an had no interest in reproducing the features of Japanese Zen monasticism, the strict and regimented training that aims at making people "forget self." In these establishments, individuality is stamped out, novices move together like a school of fish, their cross-legged posture corrected with an ever-ready stick. For Sokei-an, real individuality, the authenticity of one's spontaneous response, was what counted. This was to be found right under one's nose in the world of human relations, in the "mind-to-mind" transactions between people. The experience of direct communication was at the heart of Sokei-an's Zen, whether in his lectures, in *sanzen* (the private one-on-one interview between master and student), or in ordinary social interactions. Sokei-an demonstrated this principle, not according to any system or under controlled conditions, but by manifesting his own present mind and bringing others into it. For Sokei-an, doing this was something natural, a function like seeing or hearing, occurring without words or thought. This was the "IT" of which Sokei-an spoke, Reality itself, which could be perceived by anyone who opened his eyes.

When Sokei-an was in Japan, preparing to carry Zen to America and to "bury his bones" in the West, a friend asked him, "How are you going to teach those barbarians?" Sokei-an replied, "I teach in silence." By "silence," Sokei-an meant what he referred to as *dharmakaya*—literally, the "body of *dharma* (truth)," the highest level of Zen teaching. Before one of his talks he said, "I beg your pardon for my slow speech. First I must think about what I am going to say in English. Then I must carry out the *dharmakaya* itself before your eyes. So naturally I cannot speak as I would read a book."

In *sanzen*, Sokei-an's face would change to what I see as soft focus. When he breathed in, everything was drawn into him and held there at intense attention, an effect comparable to the instant when the conductor at a concert raises his baton before the first note. Heightened awareness was to be cultivated rather than peace of mind, or tranquil vacuity. "I shout to wake you up," he would say. The state of attention he sought was like that of a cat at a mouse-hole, a cat that is not sleeping but is relaxed and alert.

Sokei-an was similar to the Sixth Patriarch Hui-neng (638–713) in China, someone whose Zen emerged as distinctly his own. And while the Sixth Patriarch presented his Zen in Tang-dynasty Chinese, Sokei-an's record is colored by having been spoken in the English he learned in America.

Sokei-an's talks reflected his personal approach to Buddhism and to Zen. Delivered extemporaneously on Wednesday and Saturday evenings during the 1930s, they were recorded by one or several of his students, a practice facilitated by his slow delivery. Verbatim notes of the lectures were taken beginning in the early 1930s and continued to be recorded until shortly before his death in 1945. Later the various sets of notes were typed and collated, and thus his words have been preserved. Sokei-an was a skilled storyteller; yet his expression always remained natural, without self-consciousness. His remarks were never contrived or prepared in advance. He simply viewed things dramatically and described them as such. "I am like an artist," he once said, "who makes pictures in the sand. I am happy doing this. In a few minutes the waves will come and erase them."

Sokei-an was born near the Konpira Shrine in Sanuki province on February 15, 1882, the son of Tsunamichi Sasaki, a Shinto scholar-priest. His biological mother, Chiyoko, had been a concubine, the daughter of a teamaster, but his father's wife, Kitako, a warm-hearted woman from the Kubota family, loved and cared for him as though he were her own child. As a teacher for the Shinto head-quarters, Sokei-an's father traveled throughout Japan. Sokei-an accompanied him and saw all of Japan during his childhood. His father died when Sokei-an was fourteen, and Sokei-an was faced with the painful realizations that he had no faith in Shinto, that he could not expect any support from the Sasaki family, and that he did not know his biological mother.

The Sasaki family had been samurai at the time of the Meiji Restoration in 1868. When the warrior class was disbanded by the new government, each samurai family was issued government bonds according to its rank. Sokei-an's father had been selling these off, and of the little money that remained, Sokei-an received nothing. Kitako was taken back into the Kubota family, and received enough money from them to support herself independently and keep Sokei-an with her. The Kubotas decided Sokei-an had had enough education (he had completed middle school), and apprenticed him to a woodcarver.

According to Ruth Fuller Everett (1892–1967), later to become Sokei-an's wife, it was from the woodcarver that

> he learned the art of carving dragons. After a year or more spent with him, Sokei-an went on a walking tour of Shinshu, a mountainous province in mid-Japan. He went from village to village, from town to town. When he reached a place where a temple was being built or repaired, he stopped and obtained work, carving dragons for the roof beams, etc. When the work was completed, he went on to another village where he heard a temple was being repaired. He spent a year in this wandering. When he returned to Tokyo he entered the art school connected with the Imperial (now Tokyo) University. Takamura Koun was his sculpture instructor. He took a great liking to Sokei-an and invited him to become his house disciple.

In the meantime, Sokei-an had learned the details of his birth. Kitako, the woman he knew as his mother, had proved unable to bear children, and his father had procured a concubine in order to continue the family name. The concubine had assumed the wife's place for two years, then left after Sokei-an was born. After she returned to her own family with a dowry given to her by Tsunamichi, she had promptly married.

According to his own account, Sokei-an found his natural mother in Tokyo when he was about seventeen. One aunt was a geisha mistress, the other a singer of Joruri, the distinctive chanting that accompanies Bunraku puppet performances. She herself had married well and was now the mother of several children. The family was more than friendly, and were ready to share their arts with him, Sokei-an having shown some talent for performing. He felt drawn to the theatrical world, and later confessed: "I wanted to become a monologist"—a Rakugo comedian.

While a student of sculpture at the Imperial Academy of Art in Tokyo, Sokei-an worked in the post office during the school holidays to help defray his expenses. Like the Sixth Patriarch a millennium before, Sokei-an's path to Zen started when he overheard certain words that caught his attention. In this instance, they were the words "subjective/objective" and "abstract/concrete," which he heard from law students who were his colleagues at the post office. A smattering of philosophy pulled him into the conversation, and one thing led to another. After a while, one of the students suggested that Sokei-an visit the Zen Master Sokatsu Shaku (1870–1954), who maintained a lay society called Ryomo Kyokai (The Society for the Abandonment of Subjectivity and Objectivity) in Nippori. This was the beginning of Sokei-an's life in Zen.

The study center, known as Ryomo-an, had been started in 1875 by the Zen Master Imakita Kosen (1816–1892) and a group of daring and innovative men. Among them were Tesshu Yamaoka (the "last great swordmaster"); Chome Nakae, one of the first Japanese students of physics; and Count Katsu, a statesman. They were anxious to establish a *zendo* (Zen center) near Tokyo where lay disciples could train to the highest standards without entering a monastery to become monks. As Sokei-an said in 1931 in the pages of *Komyo,* the Japanese-language newsletter he published in the early years of the Institute: "Within the Japanese priesthood, the true practice of Buddhism had atrophied, and the way to rescue it was by recruiting talented people from society at large."

At Sokatsu's *zendo,* the students practiced meditation. Sokatsu received them in his *sanzen* room, one by one, morning and evening, and they had to pass his koans. (Koans are particular questions or statements given to Zen students to which they must respond in order to demonstrate their insight.) Once a month there were intensive retreats, called *sesshin,* that lasted about a week. The master would give *sanzen* four times a day. During school holidays, longer periods of practice in the *zendo* would be undertaken.

Sokei-an visited Sokatsu's *zendo* as often as he could. In his own words, he had become "a no-good boy for daily life." In this period, young Japanese men who possessed an inquiring mind might go to Paris or to Berlin to mingle with others of their kind. But Sokei-an had not learned French or German. He had, however, studied English, though it was difficult for him to speak it.

"[When] I joined the Ryomo-kai [in 1902]," Sokei-an recalled, "it was the eve of the Russo-Japanese War, and the country was in turmoil . . . . I found myself much troubled and spent this period of my life in an agony of confusion, concerned over the fate of our nation." In April 1905, at age twenty-three, Sokei-an graduated from the Imperial Academy of Art. Before he had received his actual diploma, he found himself in the army, transporting dyna-mite at the front in the Russo-Japanese War.

The war ended in the spring of the following year, but demobi-lization was slow. Returning from Manchuria as a corporal in the transportation corps, Sokei-an was inspired to try out his recently acquired showman's skills. He began entertaining the soldiers, painting scenery, devising shows, and performing in them. Remembering performances he had seen during his brief foray into the theatrical world, he mimicked set-pieces from Kabuki and Noh. "An Acolyte at the Cherry Blossom Festival" was a favorite. Back at Ryomo-an, Sokei-an showed his "act" to Soen Shaku (1859–1919), Sokatsu's teacher, who laughed aloud when he saw it as a visitor to a temple party.

This was Sokei-an's second meeting with Soen Shaku. At the first meeting, informed that Sokei-an was a sculpture student, Soen had said, "Carve a Buddha statue for me when you become a famous artist." When they met for the second time, Soen had not forgotten, and demanded, "Have you commenced to carve the Buddha statue?"

Soen Shaku was Kosen's most brilliant student. His education included not only traditional Buddhist theory and Zen training but Western science and philosophy, as well as two years following the Buddha's path in Ceylon as a barefoot monk. After taking part in the World Parliament of Religions in Chicago in 1893, Soen decided he wanted to introduce modern Buddhism to America. His message to the World Parliament was a description of Buddhism as Soen hoped it would evolve, an idealistic universal religion based on the law of cause and effect (the law of nature), and appropriate for the twentieth century. He believed that people were looking for something apart from the established religions—a church without restrictions. They wished to get hold of the essentials of religion, which are not named "God" or "Buddha" but can be understood as a spiritual force. Soen's first trip to America was enough to show him that hope for the future of the world lay in changing people's attitudes. His proposals were negotiation, universal brotherhood, and the observation of natural law.

In May 1905, Soen returned to the United States as a guest of the Russells, a wealthy American couple. For nine months he taught them about Zen in their home. In return, Mrs. Russell would give him daily English lessons so that he could communicate better with Americans.

Soen did not hesitate to enlist others to achieve his goals. D.T. Suzuki (1870–1966), a student he had inherited from Kosen, had been dispatched to America by Soen in 1897 and was hard at work preparing translations from the Chinese, editing, typing, and keeping house for the publisher Paul Carus. Now he would go on a lecture tour with Soen and prepare his talks for publication in English. Suzuki also embarked on his own career, which would continue non-stop until his death at the age of ninety-six.

Nyogen Senzaki (1876–1958), a monk of mixed Russian and Oriental parentage and a student of Soen and Kosen, joined Soen, seeking funds to support a Japanese kindergarten he had established for orphans. He worked for the Russells for a while, then went on to become a respected and creative Zen teacher. Senzaki followed Soen's "modern" style of presenting classic koans and inspired haiku. He intensely disapproved of the Japanese religious establishment.

In the spring of 1906, Sokatsu, preparing to go to America to open a branch of the Ryomo-an in San Francisco, asked Sokei-an to join him. "One day my teacher summoned me to the *hojo* [living quarters of his teacher] and said, 'I am going to America. Will you come with me?' I answered, 'I should like to go, if my mother will permit me.' 'I shall speak with your mother about this,' he said."

Sokatsu's party to North America included a student named Tomeko. It was considered improper for an unmarried woman to travel unaccompanied by family, so Sokatsu suggested Sokei-an marry her. Her family, from Sakhalin, was in the salt-from-seawater business. After obtaining his mother's consent, Sokei-an agreed to join the party and to marry Tomeko. She was vivacious and attractive, and although it was a marriage for Sokatsu's convenience, Sokei-an appears to have been not at all unwilling.

The party sailed for America on September 8, 1906. They disembarked in Seattle in October, then took the train to San Francisco. Zuigan Goto (1879–1965), Sokatsu's senior disciple, had been a philosophy student and knew English. He read in the newspaper about a farm property in Hayward, California, which Sokatsu decided to buy. It was a year before Sokatsu's party realized that they were not cut out to be farmers and moved back to San Francisco. Sokei-an had reached that conclusion when the commune's first produce elicited laughter from the professional farmers at the market. When he expressed this view, he was temporarily expelled from the group. He then entered the California Institute of Art at San Francisco, and was accepted as a student by Richard Partington, a well-known local artist.

When Sokatsu opened a Zen center on Sutter Street in San Francisco, Sokei-an returned to the fold. By 1910 the members of Sokatsu's pioneering party were ready to return to Japan—everyone except Sokei-an and his wife. Sokatsu left Sokei-an with the words: "North America is the place where Buddhism will be spread in the future. You should stay here and familiarize yourself with the attitudes and culture of this land. Be diligent! If in the future no one else appears, the responsibility for bringing Buddhism to America will be yours."

"Orientals" were not welcome in San Francisco in 1910. Even in his painting classes at the California Art Institute and at Partington's studio, Sokei-an noted instances of prejudice. On the streets, trolley cars would not stop for "yellow" faces. People who were asked for information might not proffer it. Pamphlets were distributed telling immigrants how to modulate their behavior: Don't look at women below the neck, don't look straight at them, and so forth.

Later, Sokei-an and his wife found friendlier people in Seattle. As for work, there was always cleaning to be done—in banks, various public buildings, anywhere there were spittoons. At a skating rink, Sokei-an would clean and then waltz with customers. He also took a job collecting subscriptions for the *Great Northern News,* a Japanese-American newspaper. He would visit rural readers and write their stories to be printed in the paper, thus insuring their interest in subscribing.

In Seattle, a second child, a daughter they named Seiko, was born in 1912. The first, a son named Shintaro, had been born in San Francisco in 1910. Sokei-an made an agreement with his wife: In winter, he would help with the children; in summer, he would travel.

"Alone in America now," Sokei-an said, "I conceived the idea of going about the United States on foot. In February 1911, I crossed the Shasta Mountains through the snow into Oregon. On the hillside of the Rogue River Valley was the farm of an old friend. He asked me to stay with him for a while. Summer came with the month of May. I began again my practice of meditation. Every evening I used to walk along the riverbed to a rock, chiseled by the current during thousands of years. Upon its flat surface I would practice meditation through the night, my dog at my side protecting me from the snakes. The rock is still there."

Following his teacher's instructions and his own inclinations, Sokei-an roamed the West, sometimes dressed as a Siwash Indian, getting to know America and Americans. He began writing a column he called "Nonsense" for the Japanese-American newspapers and various journals in Japan under his Buddhist name Shigetsu, meaning "finger pointing to the moon." "If I called it Buddhism," he remarked, "they wouldn't read it." His writings earned him considerable popularity, and one of his books went into four printings in Japan.

In 1916, with a third child on the way, Sokei-an sent his wife and children back to Japan to live with his ailing mother. Shortly after, he took a train to New York. He spent his first night at the Great Northern Hotel. The next day, he found a job repairing furniture and *objets d'art*, which would remain his one sure means of livelihood in the years to come.

He spent his spare time in Greenwich Village associating with writers and artists, much as he had done in his student days in Tokyo. These were years passed, he once observed, "in emptiness." He was seen dancing in the moonlight under the Washington Square arch, and translating the Chinese poems of Li Po with Maxwell Bodenheim in a café. And then he took up with a woman from a Southern family who wrote pulp fiction. She told me once how angry it would make Sokei-an when she easily passed the koans he had struggled with under Sokatsu.

Throughout this whole period, wherever he was, Zen was never absent from his mind. In Oregon, he had meditated on a rock under the stars with his dog by his side. In Manhattan, his tracks covered the city—the parks, the Battery, Sheridan Square.

In 1919, Sokei-an returned to Japan to see Sokatsu at Ryomo-an. There was one thing, he told Sokatsu, he thought he could teach

Americans after spending more than a decade in America and getting to know the people. He knew his face was the wrong color. He knew his speech was slow. But he had IT. By IT, he meant *dharmakaya*. But Sokatsu's smile told him he wasn't ready. Sokei-an recalled:

> Once again I studied under my teacher and received his fearful "shouts and blows." Suddenly experiencing *satori*, I transcended the duality of delusion and enlightenment in the great ocean of Bodhidharma's teaching. I thereupon received my teacher's *inka* [the written sanction or "seal" of enlightenment]. Because my affinity with North America was truly deep, my teacher once more sent me across the ocean. I labored hard and came to penetrate the innermost mind of the people of this land. Later [in 1926], I again returned to Japan on my teacher's orders. Some unfinished business had remained from our last encounter, and I was able to clear this up so that I could finally feel confident.

In his whole career, with some fifteen hundred or more students, Sokatsu ordained only a handful of masters, of whom Sokei-an was one. In 1926, thinking he might die soon, Sokatsu sent for Sokei-an to come "10,000 miles" to see him a second time. There was something about "absorption" that was not quite right. It was to be the last round between Sokei-an and his teacher, and it was, Sokei-an once said, "like the mating flight of hawks high in the air."

In July 1928, Sokatsu put his "seal" on Sokei-an's attainment and repeated his charge: "Go to America in my stead and spread the true teaching of Buddhism. Your responsibility is very grave. Take care!" Sokei-an said, "As a sign of the transmission, he gave me a fan which had been used by his teacher, Soen Shaku."

Referring to his transmission from Sokatsu, Sokei-an observed, "The Buddha Soul school has twenty-five hundred years of history in the Orient. In that time, it has remained the essence of our human civilization. All those in the Orient who have received the transmission of the teaching must protect it and not fail to spread it throughout the world. My own mission is to be the first to bury his bones in this land and to mark this land with the seal of the Buddha's teaching."

On April 8, 1928, Jusaburo Iwami, a friend of Sokei-an's, sent to Sokatsu in Japan a letter of appeal requesting that "Shigetsu Sasaki" teach in America. In his letter, Iwami wrote: "We know the reputation of Shigetsu Sasaki . . . who once taught here and inspired enthusiasm among Japanese as well as American Buddhists, and they were deeply impressed with his splendid teachings. His vast knowledge of English, Sanskrit, Chinese, and Japanese languages, coupled with his remarkable understanding of social conditions in this country, fit him for a return to this country in this capacity." By August, Sokei-an was in New York.

Sokei-an's career as a Zen master began in 1930, at 63 West 70th Street in New York City, when, as he put it, "I took off my hat, sat down on the chair, and began to speak Buddhism."

Sokei-an's talks at that time were designed to let Americans know everything they needed to appreciate Zen. He selected two texts as springboards into the world of Buddhism, and he spent about ten years working on English translations of them—the Sixth Patriarch's *Platform Sutra* and the *Record of Rinzai,* both classic Chinese Zen texts written about human beings, and framed in the language of ordinary people. Sokei-an spoke from these texts, commenting sentence by sentence, explaining or pointing out their special features. He also delivered informal talks, general introductions to Buddhism and to Zen, each complete in itself. It is from these lectures that the present collection has been compiled.

None of Sokei-an's talks were written down by him, but there were several official note-takers who attempted to record every lecture verbatim, even adding suggestive details to convey something of the atmosphere at Sokei-an's meetings. Parts were often "acted out" by Sokei-an in a way that transcended the spoken words. Some actors can do this, but when a Zen person does it, it assumes a dimension not often realized in the theater. Sokei-an had an atrocious accent, but a fine voice. He would do people, animals—even rocks, rivers, and oceans—all animated by his own vital energy.

In addition, Sokei-an conducted koan study. To pass koans with Sokei-an, one had to be able, like him, to be "absorbed" into objects, people, or animals. To "catch on" to Zen is something like the way a baby or animal must learn—wordlessly, face-to-face, heart-to-heart, mind-to-mind. You can do this with babies or animals. If you are "giving out"—that is, radiating—love, they know it immediately. This is unconditional love, the nourishment a mother gives her baby.

Sokei-an would play at this with me and my young women

friends who came to the Institute in the late thirties. We used to visit with Sokei-an after the meetings. We would store the chairs, wash the tea-things, and sit on the floor. He would change out of his robe, carefully put it away, and join us. Everything and anything might be a subject of conversation, but particularly we would talk about the people who came to the meetings, other members, and ourselves. Every detail of human behavior would be scrutinized.

Zen was always around, though we never mentioned it. We loved to watch Sokei-an ceremoniously remove the outer part of his priest's robe, starting with the belt, an elaborately knotted rope. Once, as he was walking toward the back of the room, where he kept his clothes, he let the end of the belt trail in front of me as I crouched on the floor. Without missing a beat, I pounced on it and caught it exactly as Chaka, his cat, often did. It would never have occurred to me to ask questions about this or that. We were simply living our own daily lives there in Sokei-an's place, and he, too, was entirely himself.

There were two signs in the room: "This Society Is Supported By Voluntary Contributions. Rules: Regular Members Monthly Contributions: $5.00. Lecture Members Monthly Contributions: $3.00" was one; and the other was, "Those who come are received; those who go are not pursued." I soon wanted to take *sanzen,* and I paid the five-dollar monthly fee to the treasurer and Institute historian, Edna Kenton. The night after I paid, Sokei-an said, "Now you are a pillar of this temple. Your donation for the year will pay one month's rent." We would count the collection on meeting nights. Sokei-an used to stand at the door as people went out and hold a bowl, monk's style, for them to put something into. Collections were terribly small. If ice cream were suddenly needed for special guests, I'd run to the corner for it. Except for Ruth, who had become a member of the Institute in 1938, none of us had money. Ruth was the daughter of a wealthy Chicago family and, before coming to the Institute, had studied Zen in Japan with a well-known master of the period, Nanshinken (1864–1935), to whom she had been introduced by D.T. Suzuki.

An era ended when we moved to the new temple at 124 East 65th Street, an establishment provided by Ruth. It was a handsome building, tastefully furnished, with one large meeting room. A few of us sat on the floor on cushions at meeting times. Others could join if they wished. The formal opening night was by invitation, the door attended by uniformed servants. It was November 8, 1941. One month later came the attack on Pearl Harbor.

Although Sokei-an regarded America as his adopted country, after the outbreak of war with Japan, he was arrested as an enemy alien and sent to an internment camp. Efforts by his American disciples to secure his release were finally successful. But Sokei-an's health was failing, and on Tuesday afternoon, May 15, 1945, at about half-past four, according to Edna Kenton's notes of that day:

> Sokei-an, stricken since the previous Saturday evening, raised himself on his bed, folded his legs, and asked that pillows be placed behind him. Sitting against them almost erect, he asked, "Am I in shape?" Then he began to talk to the three with him: Ruth on a chair at the right, Sakiko on a chair at the left, and Edna on the left edge of his bed at the foot. To his left was a large long window overlooking the little garden. His head was slightly inclined toward it. He said a few words about how to work on koans. Then in a low strong voice, very slowly and with long pauses, he said, "You must consider very intensely what you are doing every moment, not depending on any other way. It is the *only* way."

Sokei-an died on Thursday, May 17th, at six o'clock.

Sokei-an did not leave any Dharma heirs—formal, designated successors. The work of the Institute was carried forward by Ruth, whom he married in 1944, after divorcing his Japanese wife. This was done so that Ruth could have his name to carry out his translation work in Japan. In 1949, she traveled to Japan, where she became abbess of Ryosen-an, a sub-temple of Daitoku-ji in Kyoto, and established The First Zen Institute of America in Japan. The First Zen Institute of America in New York, meanwhile, continued under my stewardship.

The talks collected here are informal, concerned with introducing aspects of Zen to American audiences. They contain a minimum of technical or specialized terms and can be easily appreciated by newcomers to Buddhism or Zen. I have selected those that I found personally most compelling and most representative of Sokei-an. Much of the material included here has appeared over the years in *Zen Notes,* the Institute's monthly publication, and in

Cat's Yawn, a collection of Sokei-an's talks published by the Institute in 1947.

The preservation of Sokei-an's spoken legacy is a task that has extended over some fifty years and involved the efforts of many dedicated people. Audrey Kepner and Edna Kenton began the recording of Sokei-an's lectures in the early 1930's. They were later joined by others, including Frieda Stern, Mariquita Platov, George Fowler, Winifred Bartlett, Ruth Sasaki, and myself. The preparation of rough drafts from the collated notes was performed by various members of the Institute familiar with the material, in particular Sylvia Shapiro, who still serves as the Institute's treasurer, and Vanessa Coward, who was able to decipher the most obscure thoughts and handwriting. Among others who have assisted at various times are Richard Baamonde, Frances Bahi, William Briggs, Edward Hackney, Peter Haskel, Brian Heald, Sol Lida, Kimo Martin, William McPheters, Kenneth Patton, James Shapiro, and Georgette Siegel. Much of the work on the current volume was done by Robert Lopez. Of course, any instances of error or oversight in this volume are entirely my own responsibility.

It is not necessary to know anything about Sokei-an's personal life to understand his wisdom as expressed in his own words. Nor is it necessary to know anything about Zen's theory or practice to receive his Dharma transmission. If you listen with your inner ear, your Zen Eye will open, and as your mind clears, your own wisdom will appear. For years people have been carrying pages of Sokei-an's words around in their pockets as well as their minds. Some of the pages are crumbling into dust. It is time to put them in more permanent form.

Now as the twentieth century is inexorably setting into the past, we can see the currents flowing steadily through the Great Ocean of Mind. Sokei-an said, "Let me speak of the Zen which is my very being." This collection of Sokei-an's talks was originally addressed to his students, of whom I was one. Through them, may you absorb something of his wisdom.

Mary Farkas

THE ZEN EYE

BUDDHA

Buddha is that even mind, even and calm, which radiates in multifold directions at once. The word "buddha" comes from the Sanskrit root "to know." Buddha is one who knows, the knower. So this present consciousness is the Buddha, the knower. We know we see, we hear, we smell, we taste, we touch. Legendarily, we say Buddha, but we do not need to think Buddha and "I" are different existences in the universe. There is only one universe, one universal power in all the world, and one universal intrinsic wisdom throughout all sentient beings and all insentient beings.

This power of knowing actually performing within us is Buddha. This is our God. We worship this. We do not bow down to worship this Buddha. We meditate upon it. We do not call its name; we do not look up to the sky or peep down into the earth to find it; it is within us. We do not know where the Buddha mind is. It is not in the brain, or in the stomach. But we know it exists. We rest in it and meditate.

Just sit down and meditate. Don't put a little tag "I" on yourself. Peel the label off, and throw yourself into the great universe. You won't feel it at once, but do it every day, and you will feel it. On a lovely spring day, sit on a park bench by the Hudson River and forget yourself. When your heart beats with the rhythm of the universe, there on a park bench you will find Buddha.

BUDDHA NATURE

Everyone thinks that Buddha is different from everyday human beings. Some Buddhists believe that Buddha has been living for a million years in the Western Sky. We have no relation to such a Buddha. We have nothing to do with the Buddha living in the Western Sky. Our own Buddha nature is Buddha. Of course, sentient beings are like orphans who never knew their own home.

Once there was a child who had been abandoned. He grew up and heard that his true home was in another village. He went to the village to find his own home. Through all the streets of the village he went, visiting every house. He went into and came out of his own home but never realized it. Every man has Buddha nature within him. Going into it and coming out of it, he never realizes it is his own Buddha nature. The child finally found his home and suddenly realized that all the neighbors living there were his relatives—his cousins, uncles, and aunts. Once in a long while, man realizes Buddha nature within himself. Then, suddenly, he realizes that his hand is the hand of Buddha—the Lotus Hand. He realizes that he himself is Buddha. There is no other Buddha in the world.

THE BODY OF BUDDHA

Your body is not bounded by the surface of your skin, you know. The sun and moon are your body. The oceans and rivers are your body. The whole universe is your body. The Buddha built his religion upon *this* mind, *this* consciousness. Sometimes you call it body, sometimes you call it God. We don't use any name for it. When you observe that your mind is as boundless as the sky, an endless universe, and your present state—*this* moment—is here . . . that is all. When you have to express yourself by speech, you must realize *it is not Zen.* All the writings are in your heart, they are inherent, the intrinsic law of your nature. You cannot find this anywhere outside yourself.

One:
    Don't talk about it. The it
than becomes something else
    Don't talk about it. It
invites in someone else's yes
or no.

Don't do it. Then there's an
actor and an act.

Be it.

A JAPANESE IN NEW YORK

I spent the whole day [December 2,1936] seeing Professor [D.T.] Suzuki off after his visit to New York, so I did not have time to make my usual translation but shall speak about something important that was on my mind today.

If I were an American beginning to study Oriental religion, I would have heard that all Oriental religions are "spiritual," and living as I do in this "materialistic" civilization, I would have certain doubts about the usefulness of such study. I do not have time to entertain myself exploring ideas; my purpose in studying Oriental religion is to appropriate its understanding for my own life. Of what use would this "spiritual" Oriental religion be in my life, in this "materialistic" existence? In conclusion, if I were an American, I would give up the idea of studying Oriental religion unless I could find a reason for doing so.

If you were to ask a typical Oriental teacher about this, he would tell you that the spiritual Eastern civilization is better than the materialistic Western civilization, and that all materialism should be wiped out. But, you would ask, what about this Western civilization? It did not happen yesterday—it also has several thousand years of history behind it.

My answer to the question is this: To take either the spiritual view or the materialistic view is to take a relative view. There are no two civilizations that can be separated by drawing a line between them such as "materialistic" and "spiritual." From the beginningless beginning, these two have been one. Also, the idea of "material" is wrong, and the idea of "spiritual" is wrong.

Matter and spirit are not to be taken from two different angles. The first thing we must understand is: What is the object perceived by our consciousness? Take a drinking glass, for example. It is an object, isn't it? You call it matter. The consciousness with which you see it is spirit, you think. But if you look down upon the object because it is material and look up to your consciousness because it is spiritual, your attitude is wrong. To observe the world in such a way is childish. If there were nothing outside, and you were standing alone in space, you would not have your consciousness, for consciousness cannot maintain its existence alone. To think that consciousness existed alone, before matter, is erroneous. If one asks

6

whether matter was first or consciousness was first, the answer is that both existed at the same time.

When your consciousness evolves—your sense organs and so on—you see IT and call it form; you hear IT and call it sound. Observed from your inner consciousness in meditation, IT is just pure, etheric space, to borrow a scientific term. Observed with the eye, IT is form and color; observed through the ear, IT is sound; through the nose, IT is smell. When we use inner consciousness, there is no sound, smell, taste, touch, or appearance. Also, there is no time, no space. When we observe this existence with our sense organs all at once, we create two existences—spirit and matter. But there are neither spiritual nor material entities.

Suppose you had no eyes, no ears, no sense organs—then nothing would exist for you. Helen Keller could not prove that her consciousness existed except through the sense of touch. Except for the remaining senses, the three worlds (the world of desire, of form, and of no form) would have been empty for her. Of course, if one had no physical body, one would have no soul, though we would not call this being dead; whether one is called dead makes no difference.(If we observe the universe with the inner organ of universal consciousness, it is empty.)We call that consciousness spiritual. When that consciousness evolves and branches out to the five senses, we call it material existence. If there were no matter, there would be no consciousness. This inner consciousness is also material. In fact, these names—matter, spirit—are just words, just nonsense. Why should we dispute, standing on one to disdain the other?

There are those who say we should wipe out this material civilization, who would advise the Orientals, who are now beginning to imitate this civilization, to stop building ships and skyscrapers, just to dig a hole and lie in it. Because this material civilization creates so much unhappiness, shall we go back to the caves and take three hours to cook our food over a smoky fire? Do you think that would be "spiritual?"

How then shall students in a materialistic country combine the spiritual with the material to their advantage? If a Japanese complains about your materialistic civilization, do you think you should say, "We beg your pardon for our terrible civilization here in the West. We are terrible people. Your tea ceremony, however, is wonderful. Please tell us about it. We will listen carefully."

The Japanese will laugh at you and think you do not know the value of your own civilization. When an Oriental comes here and says you must wipe out the machine, he doesn't know what he is talking about. It is not materialistic to use machinery. To actually have a "material" society would mean that nature had not passed through the mind. When nature has not been thrown into the melting pot of the human mind and molded into a solid shape or form like a city, it is just "material." The wide plains, the miles of virgin country with no cattle, no fish—that is material, because it has not been touched by the human brain, has had no association with human beings.

This is the "spiritual" civilization you are looking for. Why not accept it? You disdain it because you have never returned to the first stage of consciousness—your original aspect—and looked at it from there. You always stand on your five senses to observe. You think you must jump out of these five windows into the sky to find the spiritual. Close your five windows and go back to the sanctuary of your consciousness. Better still, keep them open and realize that you have this inner consciousness. While you are talking or philosophizing about names, you are not in the spiritual body. Forget all these names and notions. Give them up and be yourself.

Spiritual people say we must give up desire—eating, or embracing another, is terrible, they say. Why should we give up desire? You think this because your understanding about your desire is not clear. It is better to think about this from the economic side. Desire is always limited by circumstances. To live in New York, you must pay a very high price: you can only satisfy your desire cooperatively with your neighbors. The civilization of cooperation really makes you develop non-ego. In order to satisfy your desires, you must develop the non-ego attitude; your desire becomes a social rather than an individual matter, therefore you find the Buddhist's non-ego. Everyone must play a part that harmonizes with this scheme of existence. From my standpoint, this New York civilization is Buddhist; we do not need to do anything more than enjoy it. I live here and I enjoy it. We do not need to wipe out New York and go back to the mountains. What is wrong is that we do not recognize *this* life. Don't disdain life, live in it. Do not live in it as though you were in a dream. You have the treasure, the great jewel, in your hand. Open your hand and look at it. I come from the Orient and I affirm this civilization and accept it. There is no error in this. The only error is that you do not know its value even though you have created it. You call it material, but it is a crystallization of the human brain, the human mind, which is really spiritual. This is my conclusion. I accept this as my existence in this life.

THE TRANSCENDENTAL WORLD

It sounds very queer—"the transcendental world." We have the world in which we are living. Where, then, is this so-called "transcendental world?" I have heard that name, you have heard that name, and you have seen many people doing peculiar things—joining their hands, meditating, shaving their heads, and putting on unusual robes. Or, perhaps, your sister has become a nun, has concealed herself in a cloister and never comes out; your parents visit her but may only see her through a little window. Or, perhaps, one day, your child suddenly walks into the woods and never returns. Or, some gentleman who wears a collar visits your home and talks and talks and asks your parents to donate money for something or other, and the next year you see a new building with a sharp roof on the corner of the next block. What are they doing? Besides eating three meals a day, sleeping at night, and working every day, why are they doing such queer things, you ask? It has no meaning for human life. They call it religion, but it looks to you as if they were crazy. You do not understand them at all.

The pastors in the churches talk to us about something we do not understand, something not related to politics, or stocks and bonds, or even education. Then they tell us there is a world that is different from this world, and they call it the "transcendental world." They confess, these pastors, that they haven't seen it yet. My father says he doesn't know what it is. My mother says she has heard of it, but that it is in a remote place very difficult for men and women to reach. I do not understand what this transcendental world is.

I was a dreamer when I was a child. I liked to read fairy tales and when I was alone I was always dreaming and mimicking a fairy who visited me. A story I read told of the existence of a fairy world. A child one day saw a beautiful butterfly and tried to catch it with a net. The child chased it, but the butterfly flew away, moving its wings very slowly. The child followed the butterfly and tried again to catch it, and again. "Oh! It flew quickly." The child was entirely absorbed in the single desire to catch it and followed the butterfly on and on. Finally, in fatigue, the child lay down and slept. When he opened his eyes, he found himself in an unknown world. His sisters weren't there, but young ladies who looked like his sisters appeared and took him to a beautiful palace garden. The garden was in the blue shadow of tall old trees, and everyone there spoke a language he couldn't understand.

People who live in this world and speak about the transcendental world think it must be like the world in the fairy tale; they wish to find it and be absorbed in ecstasy. So they go to church on Sunday morning and listen to the pastor's sermon and sing hymns. Their voices vibrate in the cathedral, and they try to realize the transcendental world within. They come out of the building, and all of a sudden the transcendental world disappears as they find themselves on the Fifth Avenue bus.

They persistently say there is another world in this world, but they cannot find it. When they do find it, they do not speak about it anymore, except to say they know it and are living in it.

"Absurd," you say. "This man is eating breakfast at the same table with me. How can he say he is in the transcendental world? If his mind, as he says, is in the transcendental world, then his mind must be living outside his physical body. I don't believe it."

What is this transcendental world? You have experienced it—seen those people going to church, burning incense, clasping their hands, singing hymns, shaving their heads, showering coins on the altar. What for? You see it actually before your eyes, and yet you cannot explain what they are doing. They consider themselves religious; they live differently from us. You say, "Myself, I eat three times a day." If you are a carpenter, "I work all day building houses. When evening comes, I go to bed—that is enough. I don't need to see any transcendental world."

In ancient days, a man went out from the city and entered the endless desert over which a camel could not pass—not even an elephant could cross it. He fasted in this desert twenty-seven days, drinking from a spring. One day, all of a sudden he was struck by the light of heaven and saw the transcendental world. He returned to town dressed in a sheepskin, calling out, "The Kingdom of Heaven is near!"

I have seen similar occurrences. In a village in Japan, a man who had been selling kindling wood from door to door disappeared one day. One of his children, crying, said: "Three years ago, a mountain monk came by. His skin was rough, his eyes were shimmering. He stopped and spoke to Papa, and later that day Papa said to me, 'My son, in three years you will graduate from school, then you can do my work.' Now the three years are up. Once again the mountain monk has come, and Papa has disappeared!" Years later the son saw his father among the mountain monks at a festival, but his father did not recognize him. For his father was living in the transcendental world. "Papa doesn't recognize me!" They saw each other, but they were living in different worlds. That transcendental world was very real to the father; the child cannot help but believe that it exists.

Yes, it exists. Yes, there is a transcendental world, and there is a way to enter it. But how do you do it?

If someone should ask me, "Have you entered it?" I would answer, "Yes." "Are you still in it?" "Well," I would say, "I haven't come out of it." "Oh, Sokei-an, you're kidding: you're here speaking to me, with your eyeglasses, your nose, your voice—how can you be in the transcendental world?" "I cannot explain it. I can only tell you that I am in the transcendental world, but you are not in it yet. I am here with you, I can see you, but you fail to see me—the man who is in the transcendental world."

Once I visited Concord, near Boston, and saw the bed in which Mr. Emerson died. As I stood beside the bed, I thought, "Here was someone in the West who also had some experience in the transcendental world."

Yes, it is true that there is one more world in this world. It is a different world, decidedly.

Your world and my world are not the same world. Your world is your own. Your world is yours and my world is mine. You have created your own world according to your own mind and senses; your mind is not my mind, and your senses are not my senses. I am living in a different world from yours. This can be proved very clearly at the Natural History Museum: the rooster is living in the rooster's world; the dog is living in the dog's world; the human is living in the human's world. The eyes of these beings, in fact all their sense organs, have different structures. The reality that stands before them is the same, but the world that appears through their senses is not the same.

I think I must sound very strange to you when I say that my world is mine, and your world is yours. We are living in a common world, that is true; but when we question carefully, you don't know my world, and I don't know yours—until you live in the transcendental world. There, every soul will agree that the transcendental world is one and the same.

People ask me sometimes: "Sokei-an, you have experienced the transcendental world, and you are still there—how do you feel?" I say: "I feel just like this. I got into it in my twenties and I have been there ever since, so I haven't much experience of the other world."

How did I get into it? Well, I shall tell you the truth. One day I wiped out all notions from my mind. I gave up all desire. I discarded all the words with which I thought, and stayed in quietude. I felt a little strange, as if I were being carried into something, or as if I were touching some power unknown to me. I had been near it before; I had experienced it several times, but each time I had shaken my head and run away from it. This time I decided not to run away, and "Ztt!"—I entered. I lost the boundary of my physical body. I had my skin, of course, but my physical body extended to the corners of the world. I walked two, three, four yards, but I felt I was standing in the center of the cosmos. I spoke, but my words had lost their meaning. I saw people coming toward me, but all were the same man. All were myself! I had never known this world. I had believed that I was created, but now I had to change my opinion: I had never been created. I was the cosmos; no individual Mr. Sasaki existed.

I went to my teacher. He looked at me and said, "Tell me about your new experience, your entering the transcendental world."

Did I answer him? If I spoke, I would return to the old world. If I said one word, I would step out of the new world I had entered. I looked at his face. He smiled at me. He also did not say a word.

Afterwards, I realized that to do this needed strong conceit. I went back home and told my mother. She looked at me and said, "I thought you would go crazy and die, but now it seems you have got somewhere." For in my seventeenth year I had come upon two words—"subjective" and "objective"—"Ha!" After that my brain flowed like water, and I became a no-good boy for daily life.

I realized that those ancient people who left home and stayed in the woods or monasteries, those fathers who disappeared from street corners with mountain monks, were expecting to get somewhere. I understood that there *is* a place you can enter and find a new world.

From the new world, I observed this world. Now, I enjoy this world very much, both in favorable circumstances and in adverse circumstances. I enjoy this world in joy and in agony. I have no fear of death. This is an easy world for me. I understand those religious people and their state of mind—what they are doing and what they are looking for.

There is only one key that opens the door to the new transcendental world. I can find no single word for it in English, but, using two words perhaps I can convey the meaning: shining trance. In that clear, crystallized trance—"Ztt!"—you enter the transcendental world. In one moment you enter, and in one moment your view becomes entirely different. Then you understand why people build churches and sing hymns and do strange things.

Yes, there is another world.

PURIFY YOUR MIND

Now when the whole world is in great turmoil, and all human beings are pursuing the fulfillment of their desires, we are very fortunate that Great Mother Nature has bestowed upon us minds that pursue something more than so-called desire, and that from our busy hours we can take time for spiritual attainment—sitting down in a quiet place and practicing meditation. When we are tired, we naturally take off our clothes and enter a cool pool or a warm bath to cleanse ourselves. But the people who do not know how to cleanse themselves just run from one place to the other, finally burying themselves under the filth accumulated by their minds and bodies.

Those who study Buddhism must understand the nature of this religion before they begin to practice it. The usual way of learning is something like putting on clothing—you *put* the knowledge on your mind. When you learn something, you accumulate this knowledge and that knowledge in your mind, and systematize these with your intellect for use as tools with which to accomplish your desire. Just as you would buy this coat and that hat, those shoes and this ring, to put on when you go out to visit your friends. But the way of learning in Buddhism is entirely different from putting something on your mind. The Buddhist way to perfect the personality is to remove something from the mind. You are not learning something attending Buddhist lectures, you are unlearning; you are trying to find the original nature of man. Just as when a woman tries to find her original face when she washes the makeup from her cheeks and lets her hair and eyebrows grow.

Our idea of man is different from yours. Our idea is that human nature is originally pure. Our minds become impure in the blind struggle of existence. In the beginning, human beings were compassionate and sympathetic, like all other animals—like cats and dogs, horses and cows. Even the tiger and lion are kind to their own. We, however, have lost that original quality and have become cruel and fierce because we have failed to live the natural way. We are very strange beings: we are kind to cats and dogs but fierce and cruel to one another. The human being is walking back and forth between the ways of four-footed beasts and demon-hearted spirits. We Buddhists discipline ourselves to eliminate this irregularity of mind. We remove our artificial cruelty and return to our own original nature. We don't need to use the knowledge learned from books or magazines or newspapers; we must unearth the original qualities of our mind, which have been covered for a long, long time. We must put our mind in the bathtub and scrape all the accumulations away. We must scrub it and purify it.

All religions in the world have this idea of purification. One of the main rituals in Christianity is the "ablution," the washing away of sin by water. Buddhism is also a religion of purification, but we do not use the words "pure" or "purification" in the usual worldly sense, as the denial of the body. Our physical body, as well as our mind, is originally pure; there is no need to deny the body in order to keep the mind pure. Do not be like the young Buddhist novice, who, after speaking to a woman, washed himself because he believed he had become filthy. It was not the woman, but his own notions that made him "impure." Purity has nothing to do with morality. Don't use the word purity in that queer sense.

Occasionally, people say to me, "You don't teach me anything. Though I have been with you for months, you don't answer my questions and you haven't given me any of the secret doctrines of Buddhism." If I could teach the "secret doctrines" to you, they would not be secret. They are secret because you must attain them by yourself. "All-wisdom," *sarvajnana*, is written in your soul. You must discover it by yourself. I cannot create a secret doctrine and put it on your mind. Take off all the things you are wearing on your mind and disclose that original wisdom.

There are many methods in Buddhism for purifying the mind, which is the original Buddha-nature mind. The first step begins immediately, from this human life. We have two original desires: one is to sustain our physical body by nourishing it, and the other is to sustain our species, generation after generation. You do not need to think of these in terms of impurity. Do you think eating is impure? Do you think generating offspring is impure? When you do not clearly recognize human nature, you attempt to accomplish these two desires blindly. Thus, you create the disturbances of human life. These two actions, eating and procreating, must be practiced with the agreement of others, that is, legitimately and lawfully. Therefore, human beings have created social law; they have established objectified laws to accord with circumstances.

Buddhist practice begins here in the world of desire (*kamadhatu*). By training in meditation (*dhyana*), you will certainly enter states that are different from those of the world of desire. *Dhyana* practice is the Buddhist method for attaining purity of mind. A method, however, is merely a means of attaining something. When you go to the Bronx, you take the subway; taking the subway is a method. But riding on the subway is not your life, unless you are a subway conductor. One who teaches the method for itself is like a subway conductor. The ferryboat man stays on his ferryboat, but not everyone has to stay there. When the teacher's mind is not clear, people make great mistakes. The priest is a ferryboat man, therefore he always practices the method—worship, meditation, teaching, giving sermons—for this is his profession. But the followers of religion need not necessarily practice twenty-four hours a day; they have their own lives. Too often they think they must do what a priest does. If everyone were to stay twenty-four hours a day on the subway, what would the conductor do? The priest's job is to take filth from your mind. When your mind is clean, you must return to your own life and business. Religious teachers do not teach this clearly. Everyone thinks that one must become a monk or a nun to be religious. This is erroneous teaching.

When you have scraped off all the filth of desire, you will enter the world that belongs to your pure sense-perceptions (*rupadhatu*)—seeing, hearing, smelling, tasting, and so forth, but mostly seeing and hearing. This "seeing" is different from hoping to get it; "hearing" something is different from running after it.

After this, you will enter the world beyond that of pure sense-perceptions (*arupadhatu*). This world has nothing to do with seeing or hearing; it is the state of pure mind.

In such a fashion, you eliminate desire first, then you eliminate the visible, illusory world. Then you enter the world of pure mind, which is mind itself. Here, the queer mind-stuff, which you have brought into your mind from outside, will be eliminated. It takes many years, but finally you will realize the original and pure nature of mind with which you were born, but which you have spoiled. This is the method for the purification of mind.

Teachers today misunderstand this method of purification and think it is something to attain, something to dress up in, as you do when you put on white underwear, white socks, white shoes, a white shirt, a white coat and hat, and so forth, and call yourself "purely" dressed. They say you must ascend higher and higher, like a kite in the spring sky. Such nonsense has nothing to do with Buddhism, or any other religion, in the true sense. Such teachers merely pile new delusions upon the old. They do not know what they are doing, and their students do not know what is being done. Come back to your own mind! There are no "higher" mental stages than the stage of your plain mind. These so-called "higher" stages are merely stages on the way back to your original mind.

This method of cleaning the mind is an old one and existed in India before Buddhism. The first thing the Buddha discovered was that we must clean the mind by taking off that which the mind wears. I don't teach you to put on anything; I ask you to take off— to take the sawdust out of your mind.

The fundamentals of the Buddha's teaching are agony (dukha), emptiness (shunyata), mutability (anitya), and egolessness (anatman). We undergo agony as long as we have desires—buying that gold watch, those white trousers, that Panama hat. But when you get them, the summer is gone and autumn has come. If you are naive and natural, Nature will put into your open mouth what you really have need of, but you—you look for something more than nature gives you. Thus, every one of you falls into the state of a hungry monster. As a result of cherishing a monsterlike mind, when you are thirsty and want to drink water, the water turns into fire. Or, when you meet a maiden whom you wish to marry, she is suddenly transformed into a harlot. Once you refuse Nature's gift, you cannot see the real thing, for you see everything with a deluded mind. What nature gives you, you deny and refuse. No one can escape this mistake; it is caused by karma, and everyone must bear it. This is agony. Agony is the first thing in human life. You want happiness, but as soon as you try to get happiness, the world becomes a dreadful place. Give up desire, and agony will go away. Nature provides many precious things.

Why do you think what you desire is very important? Because you think this world is really existing. When you see this object, and when you hear this sound, you attempt to grasp it, and when you have grasped it, you do not know what to do with it. Your hand is so small, while what you have grasped is as immense as the sky. Meditating and philosophizing, you will finally discover that the whole world is Emptiness. It is the base of everything. You cannot doubt it.

If you understand this Emptiness, you realize that everything is mutable. It is like a cloud in the sky that changes its shape as you look at it. I was a young man yesterday; I am an old man today; tomorrow I shall be a dead man. Nothing retains its shape. Why stick to something that is always changing? You can't hold on to it forever—everything is mutable. The power that moves the universe is bigger than the human hand. When people try to grasp it, the struggle is on.

Then, what is human? What quality in you is human? Do you think because you eat, you are human? *Pretas*—hungry spirits—eat one another, but a *preta* cannot be called human. Do you think because you procreate, you are human? All animals procreate, but an animal cannot be called human. Because you think, do you call yourself human? But this thinker is not yourself. You are just tracing the way of thinking with your words. Words are not human. There is no one who has ego in this world. A human being is only a two-footed body. Ego exists temporarily, but not as a final unit. Non-ego—*anatman*—is the final decision.

Clean up your notions. Wipe the filth from your mind. Return to your non-leaking mind, which is not ego-mind. Then you will discover, by yourself, the field of life that is extending before your eyes.

As a fundamental rule, we must meditate upon agony, emptiness, mutability, and egolessness. I have been teaching Buddhism in this house for many years, but I have never taught anything other than these four principles that the Buddha set forth when he founded his religion.

BUDDHA'S WISDOM

The Buddha's enlightenment is the origin of Buddhism. This teaching called Buddhism is based upon the Buddha's highest wisdom. It is written in the Buddhist scriptures that on the morning of December 8th, twenty-five hundred years ago, under the Bodhi tree at Buddhagaya in the kingdom of Magadha in India, the Buddha attained Awakening (*bodhi*) and All-wisdom (*sarvajnana*). All-wisdom is not the knowledge of all of the departments of science and sociology, or of philosophy and theology. Though as a child, I superstitiously thought that he had attained all this knowledge—something impossible for a human being. All-wisdom is not the so-called wisdom we can have; it is not the wisdom with which we gather knowledge of objective existence.

Of course, when a Buddhist priest opens his mouth, he immediately divides the world into two pieces. Usually he uses terms such as phenomena and reality, or inside and outside. I think you know how disinterestedly Orientals view the outside.

The outside is like a dream. It is always mutable; nothing is stable. Anyone who seeks truth on the outside is like someone trying to get milk from a male goat. Everything on the outside periodically takes on different phases, and these phases are continually changing. Therefore, there is no truth on the outside.

Then, what is on the inside? Truth must be on the inside. Well, the inside exists corresponding to the outside. When the outside does not exist, how can the inside exist? There is a famous expression in Buddhism: "Outside is empty, inside is empty; inside is empty, outside is empty; everything is empty." Well, if everything is empty, we don't need to be bothered. Good-bye, Buddhism. Many people take this attitude.

But to "be empty" is the aim of discipline in Buddhist practice. You use a different word for the same idea: you don't say "empty" your mind, you say "purify" your mind. We say "be empty." These words indicate our different conceptions of the human mind. You think that if you become "pure," you will be serious; if you become "empty," you will be stupid—an idiot. The mind of an infant is pure and empty, but the mind of an infant is also dark; it is like a black diamond. By our efforts, we must make it pure and empty like a transparent diamond.

As a first step in the practice to attain this empty mind, Buddhists, as I have said, divide everything into two pieces: inside and outside, phenomena and reality. All-wisdom does not have much to do with the phenomenal side, but it has a great deal to do with the side of reality. Usually people think that the phenomenal side exists outside, and that reality exists inside; but in the state of Reality there is neither inside nor outside. All-wisdom is the wisdom that realizes the state of Reality.

In our youth, we practice meditation to attain Reality. Entering a mountain cave, staying all summer and eating only once a day, we close our eyes and try to forget everything. When we meet the teacher, he says: "You say you have met Reality? Prove it!" But how do we prove Reality when it doesn't exist in this phenomenal world? We are still sticking to two sides; our attainment is not true attainment. Reality must be attained at this moment. It is not necessary to close your eyes; it is not necessary to keep your eyes open. It is useless to hibernate in a cave; it is also useless to run around a city block. At this moment, sitting here, you must attain Reality.

Do you think Reality can be attained with your eye? The eye creates color. Do you think Reality can be attained with your ear? The ear produces sound. You must realize that this is also a Buddhist way of speaking. Buddhists do not say, "The eye sees color, and the ear hears sound"; we say, "The eye produces color, and the ear produces sound." Wisdom, however, attains Reality. How? The answer to this question, *how,* is written in the scriptures. There are 5,048 volumes translated into Chinese; we have the answer there. This *how* is written down. But even if we spend our lives reading the scriptures, we are still far from attaining Reality.

We don't need to read all those sutras. We must attain Reality at this moment, immediately. THIS is the state of Reality. You don't need to look around. You don't need to puzzle your mind. Zen masters use the expression: *"Kachi issei!"* ("Kaah!") It is not necessary to wait many years. In this moment you must attain Reality. Then you can open your eyes to all branches of science, all schools of philosophy and theology. You can acquire the knowledge of economics, law, politics, criminology, sociology, and so forth. You can become acquainted with literature, so that you understand the

emotional life of human beings, the painful struggle of human existence, in sympathy and tears. Then you are a mature human being.
  While you are struggling to attain Reality, you are still a child,
you are only half-grown. But when you have attained Reality, your
wisdom will expand, the "seed of wisdom" will flower, will open
eight petals, embracing all the knowledge of the world. Therefore,
we call this wisdom "All-wisdom." The Buddha attained the "seed
of wisdom" on the morning of December 8th, twenty-five hundred
years ago.
  This "seed of wisdom" is like the center of Columbus Circle,
from which eight different avenues diverge. If you do not attain this
"seed of wisdom," you will spend your life going from branch to
branch without ever finding the center of wisdom. You cannot be
simple, therefore your mind cannot be plain. You think that you
must be wise, that your brain must be like an encyclopedia, that
your eyes must be shining, and that you must make all kinds of ges-
tures. No, you only need to grasp the center of wisdom.
  When we are talking about this center of wisdom in Western
terms, it is called epistemology. Of course, to understand epistemology, you must understand ontology. But the Western approach
seems peculiar to us in the East. Epistemology in the West exists
only on the blackboard, and ontology is there, too . . . but that is
not the way to find the center of your wisdom. In the West everything is objectified, while in the East everything is subjectified.
Neither approach is correct.
  When I was young, I admired people who collected many
books, who had books in every room of the house. They must have
wonderful brains, I thought, to read all those books. But now I realize such people don't read the books, because they don't have the
time. When they have the desire to read, they pick up a book and
read for about twenty minutes, then shut it and go to another. They
are certainly busy!
  I have 5,048 volumes of Buddhist sutras. When I sit down in my
chair and think about them, I realize I will never finish reading
them all in my lifetime. How can I? I spent four years reading
through the encyclopedia and ruined my eyes. Yet knowledge is
endless. There are so many things to be read; books are published
in a flood every day. If I study philosophy only, I won't have time to
study law, medicine, politics, strategy, or tactics.

I realize I must grasp something which is the center of them all. If I have the time, I shall go around, but in my lifetime I must be satisfied with this center of All-wisdom, which the Buddha attained long ago.

I am trying to simplify my life, to be a simple man, a plain man. To become a mere human being is what I am striving for. To anyone who meets me, I look like a country man. "Good morning. How do you do?" That is all. So my aim is to simplify. I am not talking about myself alone; everyone studying religion will come here in the end. Buddhism teaches this to everyone. You say Buddhism is a philosophy, a tedious and awful philosophy. Yes, it is a philosophy, but a philosophy that is like a towel that scrubs off your filth. When the filth has been scrubbed away, you will see your hand—a pure, plain hand. Buddhism is plain and simple. There is nothing complicated in it, nothing to give us a headache.

THE KEY

In India the sages left home in order to attain enlightenment and enter the absolute. Until Ashvaghosha began the teaching of Mahayana Buddhism in the first and second centuries, Buddhism was not concerned with human life. Buddhism before Ashvaghosha abominated human life and tried to retire from it. There was no opportunity to speak about love among human beings. Of course, that was not true Buddhism. When you hear the early stories told by the Buddha, you realize how simply and kindly he spoke about compassion and sympathy. But in early Buddhism, especially that which was followed by the monks, deep compassion and a conception of love were missing. They emphasized Nirvana so strongly that they forgot about human beings; they forgot about love. Christ came and completed the side that Buddhism did not touch.

Living in the West for so many years, I am convinced that Christianity is still alive in your veins, in your blood, and in your social life, though perhaps the churches have forgotten it. Even though people hate each other, it is still love that they experience.

When we observe people loving each other and hating each other, we must realize that both are expressions of love. Without strong hatred, there is no strong love. Both are included in the one word "love." In the West, the expression of it is so extravagant and so extraordinary that the Oriental could never dream of it. Of course, we have our own terms that have a similar meaning— Mahamaitri (Great Compassion) and Mahaprajna (Great Wisdom)—the mother and father of love.

The Buddha's teaching takes an entirely different direction from that of Christianity. The Buddha's direction is Emptiness, that is the part not revealed by Christ, or thought of by his disciples, or by Christians in general. Christ did not talk about Nirvana or Emptiness. Love that does not come from Emptiness is merely partiality; it is not pure at all. If it does not come from Emptiness, it is selfish love. Love that comes from Emptiness is the love of pure being, not of selfish being. Buddhism emphasizes the power of wisdom—of knowledge—more than love. Wisdom is intrinsic to all sentient nature. The power of knowing is natural and intuitive; it cannot be created. For example, I am aware of my own existence, but weeds and trees are not aware of their own existence. Theirs is a latent knowledge. Babies, as well, are without awakened wisdom. In other words, they have no consciousness of their own existence; they are sleeping. However, they will awake. What is the most important power of the human being? The power to know. I know you are here; you know I am here; you have done this to me—it was harmful, but you know it.

No one can invent love. Love is a natural power of the human being. No one can counterfeit love by willpower. Love has no egotistic attitude, for the egotistic attitude has no love—it has desire but no love. Love is like a bird in a cage—it sings! It has no desire. What makes a bird sing? It is love.

Christian love, like the wisdom of Buddhism, is also non-ego. You admire love between man and woman because you cannot create it by willpower. A man and a woman meet and fall in love because it is natural. You cannot buy love with money, you cannot obtain it by willpower; therefore, it is wonderful and sacred. If you try to buy it with money, you desecrate the whole of love and it will be broken into pieces. All things that cannot be desecrated are wonderful—such as the wisdom with which we see, hear and understand; the love through which we unite and come together; and the courage to fight for life. Love is the essential element binding together all sentient beings.

In the early period of Greek philosophy, they thought each molecule had some kind of hook by which it linked itself with other molecules. Without this hook, nothing could maintain its force, nothing could maintain its own existence. They thought that each molecule was a link in the chain of material existence, and that each link had a hook to engage with other links. Today, scientists say it is electricity that provides the cohesiveness that forms matter.

From a religious standpoint, the power that brings human beings together is love. Without it, there is no society, no family. This love is a wonderful instinct in all sentient beings—not only human beings. Even ferocious tigers love with a mother's love, a child's love.

Two thousand years ago, Christ spoke the word "love" aloud, and people's minds awoke. Love, in its purity, freed their minds.

I am happy that I, one human being, understand these two wonderful religions of the East and West, whose common basis is non-ego.

In love, you and I are one. When I say something, you are

speaking the same thing. When you say something, I am speaking the same thing. We are not in love with *each other*. In love, you must not recognize yourself: you are he. He must not recognize himself: he is you. Both are completely united. There are no two persons. There must be one person.

If I were to explain what non-ego is, I would use the same words. Non-ego does not destroy the person; it supports everything and is supported by the whole. Love is the same. Christianity is the religion of love. Buddhism is the religion of wisdom. The Oriental attitude of non-ego is the Christian attitude of love. Without love, wisdom is like a sword that destroys but cannot create. Love without wisdom is like a fire that burns everything and does not give life to things. Love and wisdom are one thing. When we take this into ourselves, it is wisdom. When we give it to another, it is love. With this one key in my mind, Christianity and Buddhism come to know one another.

I did not discover this secret for a long, long time. It was my mission to grasp something that was common to the East and West. I had thought that if I could find this key, I could open all the secrets of both hemispheres. Comparing Eastern and Western philosophy, including early Buddhism and Greek philosophy, I failed at first to discover the key that would open both sides. Finally, I found the key—one key with two names: love and non-ego. I had found the priceless jewel.

I came to this country with my teacher when I was twenty, and stayed for twelve years. I went back and forth several times. This time I have been back for nine years, and have been observing the heart and life of the people of the West.

I have stayed in this country for a long time. I felt I had completed my mission by finding this key. Those who do not pay attention to thoughts think my discovery means nothing; it has no more value than a cultured pearl. But those who study the thoughts of humankind will certainly accept my discovery as a key with which to open the treasure chest that holds the secrets of the East and of the West. Those who are only concerned with earning money or building cities do not place much emphasis on thoughts. But human beings live in thoughts. They are the only treasure human beings possess.

I am a student of thoughts, and those who come here are students of thoughts. I rejoice in having the opportunity to announce this discovery. The one who first announces this discovery is myself, Sokei-an.

THE OUTER HOUSE AND THE
INNER HOUSE

The objective world of appearance and the subjective world of mind are the outer and inner houses wherein our soul resides. As thinking men and women, we must thoroughly acquaint ourselves with our two kinds of houses.

We know quite well that this outer house is not really an existence. This red stick on my lecture table, for instance, is a part of the outer house; you say its color is vermilion. This cushion is also a part of the furnishings of the outer house; you say its color is green. But color does not exist in either the cushion or the stick; color has its existence on the retina of your eye. The sound of this gong is created on the drum of your ear; there is no sound in the gong itself. Taste is produced on your tongue. It does not exist in food. I do not need to explain more carefully, for science proves this.

Then what is the reality of outer existence? A philosopher may say, "The reality of outer existence is noumenon." But what is noumenon? The philosopher explains it as existence that has no relation to the five senses. You ask: "Then how can we know that it exists?" The philosopher answers: "By our intellect we know that noumenon exists, but with our five senses we perceive it as phenomenal existence." The blue sky, the green water, the pink flowers—these are only phenomena; they are the appearances of reality, not reality itself. When I was young and studied Western philosophy in school, I was amazed. I thought, "Western philosophers are thinking with our Buddhism!"

Since we are living in this strange outside house, which is not a real existence at all, and since we cannot do anything about it, we have to accept it as it appears to be.

We heap up fragments of phenomena, giving them names such as iron and stone, tile and concrete, and fashion them into shelters for our physical bodies to live in. We harbor fear for their loss; we bewail their changeable nature, and hope against hope for their eternal existence. We clutch at those appearances that are our most cherished possessions and weep bitterly when they vanish. The outside house is truly a very unreliable existence.

The physical body, which in old-style thinking consists of earth, water, fire, and air, is also merely an appearance. As the Buddha said, it is born, remains a while, decays, and disappears. This physical house, the human body, is more fragile than the house created out of iron and stone, tile and concrete. But it is my own dear house! I only have this one; I have no other. I guard it as a treasure—this body that seems to be mine, yet really is not.

By thus carefully observing the outside house, we naturally come to realize that we live also in an inner house. What is this inner house? Of what is it composed? Your soul lives in the inner house, just as your body lives in the outer house. This inner house is made up of thoughts, dreams, and mental images. Mental images are its bony structure, thoughts its flesh, emotions its nervous system, intellect its arteries, and consciousness its heart. This inner house, like the outer house, is also phenomena, and is as shaky as the outer house. If you close your eyes to the outside house and turn your attention within, you can see what kind of dwelling is this inner house you live in. From morning to evening the dreams and notions of which it is composed pass before your inner eye like the silhouettes of a procession of demons. Do you realize this?

Every one of you lives in such an inner house. Some inner houses are constructed according to systems: Christianity, Buddhism, Transcendentalism, Greek philosophy, the school of Immanuel Kant. Many people, to be sure, do not live in inner houses constructed according to systems, but live in houses made of weeds and straw and bamboo, houses without pillars or roofs. Those who live in magnificent outer houses, costing millions of dollars to build, may have only a hovel as an inner house. But there are others who have beautiful inner houses decorated with gems garnered through the ages—the ideas of Plato, Schopenhauer, and Hegel, for instance. They have cut out lines from Emerson and Longfellow and Whitman and hung them on the walls of their inner houses to keep their minds in order. Some live in modern houses: Democracy, Socialism, Communism. Others live in foreign houses such as Sufism, Bahaism, Buddhism, Vedanta, or Zen. Just as you Americans build foreign houses to live in, so you live in foreign thoughts. If you find them a little awkward to live in, you make a slight alteration and adapt them to your needs, calling them Buddho-Christology, or some such name. In such a way we create our inner house and live in it.

In the Orient there are wonderful inner houses. In Buddhism, for instance, there is the *Flower Garland Sutra,* the *Lotus Sutra,* and the *Vibhasa Shastra.* This last is so magnificent and so beautiful that to go through it from end to end, one must spend one's entire lifetime! These are truly pyramids of human thought; they are wonderful houses in which any human being can reside without ever growing weary of their beauty and dignity. They give us a system of thought by which we can live and within which we can find rest.

But, after all, even these are nothing but houses, temporary existences. Today we can visit the pyramids of Egypt. They were the outer houses of the Egyptians. In what inner houses they were abiding is not very clear to us now, but they had their own wonderful religions, their own strange faiths, such as the worship of Isis and Osiris. Would that we could realize these again! But these inner houses are also phenomena—fragile, mutable, and ephemeral, passing before our soul like wreaths of smoke, continually changing like clouds and sunshine. If you try to keep them, you will realize their nature: they appear, they remain, they decay, and they disappear. Shakyamuni Buddha told us that everything that exists passes through these four phases—growing, remaining, decaying, and passing away. To watch the changing phases of our mind-houses brings us agony, brings us tears, as we cry, "Don't go! Don't go!" Nevertheless, they go.

We cannot keep our outside house forever, nor can we keep our inside house forever. Therefore, we must know with our intellect when the change takes place; we must realize the impossibility of escape from the agony that arises when one thing changes its form and becomes another. The thoughts of the eighteenth century do not exist now; the thoughts we have today will not exist in our great-grandchildren's day. The conceptions of life become different. Therefore, we must break our attachment to both the inner and outer houses. You say, "Well, it is fun to live in them. When I was young I enjoyed my young body; now that I am old, I cherish my old body. Yesterday, I enjoyed my young notions; today, I am very happy to have my mature ideas. I don't mind accepting this agony. Though I am tortured by these transitions and though I fall into hell holding these ideas, I shall cling to them. This is my decision." Well, it is your decision, no one can say you mustn't.

But do not think of this as just a lecture. You must really think carefully about the kind of house you live in. Do you know the entrance to your house? Do you know the exit? Do you know how many windows it has? Perhaps you have lost yourself in it. You have to know exactly where you are in your inside house; it is important to your entire life.

Like those who don't build outside houses, if you don't build an inside house, you are like the foxes and badgers that live in caves or holes in the earth. They are not human beings. We must have an outside house.

Just as we must have a physical body to exist, we must have a solid inside house as well. For an outside house to exist for two hundred years, you must have a solid foundation of strong materials. We can keep this body for just a hundred years, at the most. (When I was young, I would have said fifty; now that I am sixty, I shall have to add a few more years.)

But the inside house is not so fragile as the outside house. Buddhism has existed for twenty-five hundred years. The house of Christianity is two thousand years old. The wonderful thoughts and philosophies of the past still exist today. Perhaps you are living in the house in which your grandmother lived. Thoughts often endure three generations. In my country there was no individuality. In olden times we denied individual existence—original human individualism was forgotten. Everyone lived as a member of a family. No child had a personal existence. No subject could claim freedom as an individual; all lived under a strict feudal regime. Today, the age of the individual has come. "My money is mine; I have the right to use it according to my own wishes." My country choked on this new idea. The young men of my grandfather's generation were always arguing: "No person has the right to use his money according to his own wishes; it is not his possession." What kind of argument was that? Now, everyone knows that my money is mine, but at that time no one knew to whom money belonged. Of course today, if you examine the situation carefully, no one really possesses his own property. But this is an economic analysis. From the common-sense standpoint, we do have possessions. In former days, however, even from a common-sense point of view, no one held anything in his own hands.

Well, we have to accept the changes to the outside house, and we have to adapt ourselves to them. We also have to adapt ourselves to the changes to our inside house. We have to undergo the agony that comes from the birth of new thoughts and from the continuance of present thoughts; we have to shriek when old thoughts are decaying and sleep when our thoughts decline. This is so-called human life, you know. We enjoy living in a city apartment with an elevator. We also enjoy going to the country where there is no sidewalk, staying in a house of stone and clay, and walking barefoot.

As long as we are living in this body, which has five senses, we cannot refuse sound, we cannot refuse color. We must accept both agony and joy. But, as a Buddhist monk, I can only say: You must not attach to them; you must have freedom of soul. You must not make a suicide pact with your inside house. The soul is alone. It lives and sleeps in these two houses. We must realize that these houses are not ourselves, but merely the houses in which the soul dwells.

THE UNIVERSE IS ANOTHER NAME
FOR INFINITE CONSCIOUSNESS

When you think of your religion, it is natural for you to think about the nature of God. When we think of Buddhism, it is natural for us to think of how the universe is created. The Buddhist thinks the universe is eternal existence; it has never been created, it will never be destroyed. You may ask: "Are you saying that the sun and moon, the earth and stars, exist through eternity and will never be destroyed or cease to exist?" The Buddhist answers: "We do not understand what you are talking about. We think the universe is another name for infinite consciousness. There is nothing in the universe but consciousness; only consciousness exists. What is this gong? Consciousness. What is this fire? Consciousness." "Then," you may further ask, "Buddhists think that there is nothing in the universe—no men, no women, no earth, no sun—that consciousness alone exists?" The Buddhist replies, "Indeed, that is our concept of the universe." You say: "Ridiculous! What are *you* then?" Opening my arms wide, I say: "*This. This* is consciousness." Having asked all your questions, you put on your coat and go.

Of course, when we borrow the English word "consciousness," perhaps our use, or our borrowing of it, is in error. Perhaps we should use your word "soul." But you think that your soul is your own soul, different from my soul, and that God created each soul individually. We do not think so. We think all existence is soul, an ocean of soul, and we are the waves. This is the Buddhist's basic concept of the universe.

Then you think: "How can this one mass of consciousness be matter and spirit? Matter exists outside, and spirit exists inside." So you ask: "You said this gong is consciousness?" "Yes. I said *this* is consciousness." "How can matter be consciousness?" I answer: "From our standpoint, *this* is not matter at all. When I strike the gong, *this* also is not matter; *this* is one side of the two halves of consciousness. When we cut a melon in two, both sides fit together. We say the outside is one of the halves of consciousness—one half of consciousness."

When I was young, I always questioned whether an object's color existed in it. It does not exist there but on the retina of my

31

eyes, because all color is created in the eyes. Then what is it that exists there in the object? According to your science, vibration exists there. The vibration of what? The vibration of ether. The rays of the sun produce vibrations, and our consciousness vibrates with them. According to the degree of vibration, color is produced on the retina of the eye, just as sound, when I strike the gong, is produced on the drum of the ear. The vibration of air, but not the sound, is produced by striking the gong. I thought Western science explained everything very clearly. I was happy to know the theory of vibration in ether and in light. Your scientists said that the things that exist around us are ether. Fundamental existence is also ether.

These days, however, scientists have changed their theory. To explain the foundation of the universe, they now use the electron theory; the electron is reality. The name has been changed. Philosophers explain that the real object that exists is noumenon, not phenomenon. Noumenon is not color, noumenon is not sound. We cannot demonstrate the shape or color of noumenon. It exists beyond our five senses, but it exists; it is real existence. Sometimes philosophers call it reality—things existing by themselves. "Well," I thought, "that is very near to Buddhism." Philosophers try to prove it. But how can they know the existence of a reality that has nothing to do with the five senses? Since it has never existed in the realm of the five senses, how can they prove it? Somehow, they explain, they have proved it dialectically. Buddhists have a shortcut to understanding this thing that has nothing to do with our five senses. The pivot of Buddhism is to understand the one thing that exists, but that is not existing in the realm of our five senses. I cannot see it; I cannot smell it; I cannot hear it; I cannot grasp it; I cannot even think about it; but I know there is such an existence without calling it by any name. Of course, Buddhists have given it many names—Emptiness, Original Nature, Buddha nature, Nirvana—there are plenty of names. Sometimes they call it Amida Buddha, or Mahavairochana Buddha. They have given it so many names, they certainly must have known it.

I woke up to that existence all of a sudden, bewildered as to what to call it. I realized later that many people have proved its existence. Well, it is not existing in the sphere of the senses, or in the sphere of the intellect. Perhaps we do not need to say anything about it, but we cannot push it entirely outside of our thinking activity, unless we are unable to think anything about anything.

When we say, "That man has attained enlightenment," we are saying that he has proven the existence of Emptiness and from that state of Emptiness can deduce all existing things. Then, when he talks about the universe, the world, and humankind, we certainly can say he has attained enlightened wisdom.

The outside is one side of this Emptiness, and the inside is the other. The outside called Emptiness is vibrating—it is living, not dead. Perhaps it is dead matter to our senses, but the thing itself is not dead; it is always living. The inside is living always, too. My death and my birth do not interfere with the perpetual existence of the inside called consciousness. When outside and inside meet, existence is produced. Until that time, there is no existence. Potentially there is, but no one knows of it. When I say "inside," it is not *my* inside. When I say "outside," it is not *the* outside I am looking at. It is the nature of consciousness to look at everything, to realize both existence and consciousness when the "concussion" occurs. Otherwise we do not call it consciousness. This is the fundamental faith, if I can use this word of the Buddhists. Buddhists do not call it God, do not call it Creation. That unthinkable existence appears under two names—matter and spirit. Man proves the side of the spirit by himself, but not until he makes contact with matter, or, to use a Buddhist word, until he makes yoga [union] with matter. Though this word "yoga" is so important, its meaning has degenerated and it is used in a very loose way today. When Shakyamuni Buddha used this word, he used it in its original sense.

The next question is: What is discernment? When we make contact with the outside, with consciousness or matter, whichever you call it—some Buddhists call it real or perpetual existence—whether *your* consciousness has proved it or not, the existence outside is *real* existence, not phenomena.

We reach this state by meditation and by the study of koans. In a famous koan, we look at a stone in the garden and ask: "Is the stone existing within us, or is it existing outside in the garden?" Thinking about such problems, we really come to the knowledge we are seeking.

After we see that this real existence is a single mass of existence, we slowly perceive the many different appearances within it. When I was motoring on Long Island, our car suddenly came upon an immense garden; three or four acres were covered with crimson tulips. You could have called it a "crimson" field. But inevitably you begin to discriminate, to see one part and then another, like an artist learning to use colors. When you first look at a landscape, you might say "pale"—the sky is pale, and the tree leaves are pale also. Later you would say the sky is blue and the trees green, and later still you would find many shades of blue and green—blue-green, yellow-green, gray-blue—you would see as many colors as you have learned, thus defining many shades. Your eye must be trained to see all these shades of color.

I study painting. In the beginning, I used only one color to paint the sky blue. My teacher, Mr. Partington, complained, "Are you painting the sky?" "Yes, I am." "Then paint the sky, don't just spread paint on the canvas." When we look at the sky, every minute the color is changing. Even as I turned to mix blue to match the sky, the sky had changed. I am sure you understand this.

This knack of seeing shades of color can be applied to seeing human life. If you say someone is bad, or someone is good, it is like saying the sky is blue—nothing can be accurate in your thinking. "Good" and "bad" are names. We look at everything with these names, and we always think about everything with these names. This is a naive and inaccurate way of thinking. Because your mother said "bad," it is bad; because your father said "good," it is good. And you teach this to your children and never think about it. Your brain doesn't work until you get into some real predicament. Then you must think about it yourself, and you must make a judgment yourself. Well, you see smoke behind your house and think there must be a fire. This proves to be accurate, so you conclude, "Where there is smoke, there must be fire." Then you see a cloud over in New Jersey that looks like smoke, and you think there is a fire. This time it is not accurate at all.

When your discernment becomes accurate, you will not make this mistake; you will know. When you come to life, you know death. When you know light, you understand shadow. When you realize enlightened mind, you can comprehend deluded mind. There is a Chinese saying: "When the women and the horses become fat, you know there is war in the future." The tree is green, but when you see the first leaf falling, you know that autumn has come.

THE GREAT OCEAN

Buddhism has two goals or aims: One is to attain emancipation—freedom from all attachment; the other is to avoid sickness and disaster by bringing peace and security to the world. The peace of the world and the security of our families is thought by Buddhists to result from our having attained freedom from all attachment.

If a king becomes *attached* to the making of battleships, this making of weapons to attack other countries will bring disaster to his own country and destroy peace in the world. If a gentleman with home ties *attaches* himself to a beautiful lady on Broadway, he breaks the peace and brings disaster on himself and his family.

Many of the fires in Japan, or anywhere else for that matter, are the result of hatred between human beings. One person, moved by hate, starts a fire in someone's house to burn it down, but in the end the wind carries the fire next door and the result is a whole city wiped out.

To achieve peace in the world, one must attain emancipation from the unnatural, that is, from attachment. In early Buddhism, to be free from attachment was the main point, the foundation of Buddhism. The Buddha taught his disciples many ways to detach themselves from unnatural desire. A very old sutra concerning this is called *Samudra,* the Great Ocean, the Big Sea.

The Great Ocean refers not only to the ocean of water, but to the atmospheric ocean, the ocean of light. When the Buddha was sojourning in the Jetavana garden, one day he said to his disciples: "What is the Great Ocean?" And he began to speak about the sea to the south of India, the Indian Ocean.

When a boat is sailing smoothly over the southern sea, suddenly there appears, on the horizon, a black dot. As one watches, this black dot spreads over the sky. It is the monsoon. The wind is black, and the rain is like ink. Those who sail the Indian Ocean see black water that doesn't stain your hand; when the rains come, the navigator meets waves black as ink, and black raindrops fall from the sky like a waterfall.

In some parts of the Pacific Ocean, after November there is not one clear day all winter. Every day, ships sail in mist and fog in a dark sea. The waves are so rough the ship seems to stand upright.

To the south of Japan, in the middle of a channel, is a great whirlpool, which even big ships do not dare approach. Avoiding it, smaller craft pass by close to the shore. One can see them from there. In the evening, so it is said, as the sailors are enjoying the bright moonlight, singing songs, and playing instruments, they will suddenly see the faint figure of a man in the dark air. It screams: "Water, give me water!" A sailor cries out: "A ghost, a ghost!" And someone flings a bucket of water into the air. For a moment the ghost disappears, but it is soon back again, pursuing the boat, crying, "Water, water!"

A monk tells them: "The sea near the shore is covered with reeds, among which many spirits of the dead wander. It is they who pursue the ships, begging for water." What are the sailors to do? "Do not throw real water to dead spirits. Knock out the bottom of the pail and throw the ghost the water that isn't there." When this is done the ghost pursuing the ship disappears, to return no more.

The Buddha did not tell this story, but he did tell many stories of the sea. He was a wonderful storyteller, and through these stories he would slowly come to the point he wished to make.

The ordinary sea, he told his followers, is the sea that anyone can comprehend. But the sea about which I am now going to speak is not a sea of water. There are small bodies of water and large bodies of water called seas, but the sea of which I speak belongs to the eye. All phenomena—appearance such as the blue sky, the green water, the brown earth—are the waves of that ocean to the eye of Buddha.

If you can tolerate and endure the waves in this ocean of phenomena, you will be able to sail safely across. When the billows toss and churn, and many demons, evil spirits, and evil insects try to harm you, if you cannot tolerate the waves, you will be lost.

Imagine the stories the Buddha may have told. The Hindus of his time believed that there were many islands in the southern ocean on which demons, particularly female demons, lived. Many stories were told about these demons. When the merchants who voyaged into the southern ocean to find pearls and other jewels disappeared, it was believed that they were caught by female demons. Ceylon was thought to be inhabited by evil spirits and crocodiles.

This is an allegorical way of speaking about the existence of this world of ours, for if you are caught and trapped and die, you cannot attain emancipation. For instance, a man's eye follows a beautiful woman. His consciousness is clouded by the lust of his eye; he loses the eye of his consciousness and falls into the whirlpool of desire.

Then there is also the ocean of sound. A young man who follows the ocean of sound begins to study music, is infatuated by the beauty of sound, plays day and night, is driven from place to place, apartment to apartment, until he is reduced to playing the violin on the sidewalk, or in the subway. According to the Buddha, he would be all right if he could swim across the ocean of sound. But if he cannot, he will drown, and end up by the East River sawing away on a street corner.

There are also the oceans of smell, taste, and touch. They are not so great and can be easily imagined—gluttony, for instance. The ocean of mind is the greatest. Really only a very few people save themselves from the tossing and churning and boiling waves of the ocean of mind. When the ocean tosses and the waves of mind blow in your brain, you do not know how to sail across, and you are lost. There are many foes in the invisible ocean of the subconscious mind. You may feel quite sure you are not indulging yourself or being carried along by the waves. But even when you don't know it, unconsciously your direction is governed by them.

Then there is the ocean of consciousness, fundamental consciousness, the bottom of mind, the *alaya-vijnana*. You think it is eternal—God. At the end of the day, when you die, there is still this consciousness at the bottom of mind. And you think you can sail across this ocean, that your soul exists. When you are in the consciousness of the bottom of mind, you think you will exist forever. Many people think we depart from this life not losing the consciousness of mind, self-consciousness. They believe that this ocean can be sailed with cognition and awareness. But when the black veil covers the eye, that faith betrays them. They drop into the empty void, the abyss of darkness. Then consciousness comes again, and again goes, and again comes. They shriek with terror. At that moment they realize complete nothingness, unawareness, absolute unconsciousness. They realize that there is no channel that reaches from them to God. They no longer believe that there is a way to find God. All their lifetime they have believed, but at the moment of death, they lose their faith. What is there for them to do?

Attain enlightenment at that moment? It's too late. They die in great doubt. The Buddha has expressed this in poetical form. In the great sea, there are evil insects and demons. The billows toss and whirl, and you are afraid. It is difficult to cross the big sea.

If we can sail across the great ocean, we annihilate all remnants of attachment forever, and will not take another body. Thus we find eternal Nirvana and never again return to our self-indulgence. When we annihilate the accumulation of desire, and clear the remains of attachment, we do not need to return. Many times we experience annihilation, many times we return to attachment before we attain complete detachment. I do not much like the term detachment. Buddha's detachment is different from selfish detachment. Buddha's detachment means detachment from selfish attitude. When you realize your own place and time, ability and capacity, you will easily get to the bottom of true detachment.

In the battlefield, I experienced detachment every morning. Every morning I ate my last breakfast. I gave up all attachment and the dream of a wonderful future. I did not suffer.

I am standing on the roadside, watching you go astray. If you ask me which way to go, I will tell you.

THE KNOWER, THE GOD OF
BUDDHISM

The God of Buddhism is the god of wisdom. In Buddhism, the Buddha means one who knows, the knower. One who knows one's own wisdom is Buddha.

Our eyes, which have the faculty of seeing; our ears, which have the faculty of hearing; our other senses—smell, taste, touch—are all manifestations of the power of knowing. So our sense organs are the eyes of Buddha. Every one of us is Buddha. However, Mr. So-and-so is not Buddha, but our "persons" are Buddha.

A Buddhist student who comes to this country to study Christianity hears Christian preachers attacking the Buddhist faith. They say that Buddhism is not, in the true sense, a religion, because Buddhists worship something abstract, some doctrine of Emptiness or Nirvana—philosophical conclusions that are not God. Christians, however, worship a personal god. They say Buddhists worship a metaphysical doctrine or notion symbolized in their iconographic images; they do not know a personal god. One young monk went back to his temple and asked his elder about this. The elder said, "We do not need to say anything about or worship our personal god, because each one of us is God *in person.*"

The Buddhist believes in a pantheistic god. This personal, pantheistic god is god-nature in me, in you, in all sentient beings—in everything. The Christian believes that human beings can achieve access to God through Christ, that those who do not know Christ cannot achieve access to Him, and that sentient beings lower than human beings have, of course, no god-nature, no soul in them. The souls that are chosen by God are the subjects of God.

This is not an easy subject for one lecture. When we talk about the attributes of God, according to Christianity and to Buddhism, we find many questions that must be asked and answered. The Buddhist thinks the person is God, but that the person is not an individual. There is no such word in the Orient as "individual"! The Buddhist believes that souls are not created by God, one by one, but that each is a drop of water in the ocean of soul. The ocean of soul is existence; it is Being existing from the beginningless beginning to the endless end. So there is no creation of the universe and no destruction of the universe. Each wave of the ocean has its own character, its own shape, its own power, and its own velocity, yet all waves are nothing but the body of water that is the sea. Each individual has his or her own keynote and characteristics, yet all individuals are nothing but waves in the ocean of soul.

We are in the habit of calling this pantheistic view of soul "Oriental." Westerners believe each individual soul was created in the past and will continue to manifest for a long, long time. This is a distinction between the West and the East. We must note this point. The West believes souls are individual; the Orient believes souls are non-ego. Of course, we in the Orient have been attacked many times by Christian missionaries for this belief. "All Orientals," they say, "are like salmon in the Alaskan sea. When one surges right, all surge to the right; when one surges left, all surge to the left. Orientals are groups of souls." Our reply to this is: "There is no opposition."

Buddhists who have awakened have awareness of their own existence, unlike weeds and trees and lower sentient beings that have no awareness. Their Buddha nature is asleep, latent. Awakened Buddha knowledge must be enlightened as Shakyamuni Buddha himself was.

Buddha means power of knowledge. Shakyamuni Buddha is the one who was born about twenty-five hundred years ago and attained Buddha knowledge through his own enlightenment. "Buddha" is, therefore, an abstract noun, and "the Buddha" is a proper noun that has deep meaning.

The Buddha consists of two elements called mind and body, Buddha and the place of Buddha, Buddha and Buddha's dominion, soul and the place of soul, spirit and the body of spirit. In your language, the spiritual side is called "spirit," and the material side is called "body." When I was listening to Christian sermons over my radio, I heard Christians also divide this human body into two elements—"body" and "spirit." The spirit is good, the body is bad. They do not understand why spirit must be mixed up with the sinful body.

In our language, we speak of the five *skandhas*. The "material" side is called *rupa*; while the "spiritual" side, mind, is divided into four elements: first is sense-perception (*vedana*); second is thought (*samjna*); third is mind-movement (*samskara*); fourth is consciousness (*vijnana*).

The second of these elements, thoughts (*samjna*), is regarded as a semi-material state of mind. Pure mind-movement is like pure water. Nature throws junk into this pure water. Debris enters through the eyes, the ears, and so on, and is all shaken up. So, whenever we think, we must use this "stuff"; we cannot think without words or vision. Words, visions, and thoughts are all *samjna*. If we keep the mind quiet through meditation, all this "stuff" will be separated from mind-movement (*samskara*). The debris will come to the top, and clear mind will show its stability. The bottom of the ocean of mind is not my mind; it is the mind of the universe. No "stuff" from the outside can reach its depths; it is bottomless. All is transparency here. The ocean is *vijnana*, consciousness itself. The creative power of the universe is not a human being; it is Buddha. The one who sees, and the one who hears is not this eye or ear, but the one who is *this* consciousness.

This One is Buddha. *This One* appears in every mind. *This One* is common to all sentient beings, and is God. We worship *This One*, therefore, we join our hands and bend our heads before *This One*. *This One* is the only one in whom we can trust; we can depend upon *This One*. We come from *This One*, and we will go back to *This One*. *This One* is always with us. *This One* is not concealed from us. We see *This One* always, day and night, and we know *This One*'s eternity, omniscience, omnipresence, and omnipotent power. *This One* is very near to us; we can speak to *This One*, and *This One* answers us. *This One* guards us. We love *This One*; we are the children of *This One*. We do not need a temple outside; we are the temple. We do not need a choir to offer *This One* hymns; meditation, when the mind is tranquil, is our hymn, which we offer. Our religion is plain and simple and true. We do not need any preacher. When we come home and sit down and join our hands in meditation, in tranquillity we realize this crystallized consciousness within us, and that is our ritual.

THE SHAPE OF MIND

Once when the Buddha was sojourning in the city of Shravasti, he put on his robe in the morning and took his bowl and went to the village to beg for food from door to door. He returned to his abiding place and finished his morning meal. Then he sat in his accustomed seat and smiled.

Maudgalyayana, one of his great disciples, said: "O Lokanatha [Lord of Worlds], I know why you smiled. I saw the same thing this morning. It was a very absurd monster, wasn't it? His body was as big as the side of a house. His face had been smashed. He was shrieking through the sky with his blood dripping behind him."

In the conversations between the Buddha and Maudgalyayana related in the Agamas [early Buddhist scriptures], there are many stories about these kinds of monsters.

I have been thinking about these monsters and trying to understand the stories about them for many years. I also see these types of monsters sometimes and smile to myself. If you were to see someone with eyes in his back, a mouth on each cheek, and only one finger on each hand, certainly you would think he was a monster or demon. But you do not realize it when you meet someone whose *mind* is in such a shape. Though he may have a perfect body and a beautiful face, if his mind is disarranged, it would be as if his feet grew from his head and his hands grew from his ears. He would be a monster or demon.

Sometimes you associate with such monsters without knowing it. Everyone knows when the body is unusual, but people fail to realize when their minds are twisted, warped, or disarranged. You must therefore understand the nature of mind—how it was created and how it can be used. Before you manicure your fingernails, you must manicure your mind; before you scrub your skin, you must wash your mind in pure water. Knowing the form of your mind is the first step in understanding the Buddha's teaching. Of course, in the West there is the science of psychology. But you are not wasting your time when you listen to how Buddhists think about the shape of mind. This evening I shall make an analysis of the formation of our minds, so that you may be able to avoid walking upside-down while you hang yourself from the sky in order to live in this world.

If you study Buddhism from books, you will not be able to find this teaching very easily. Usually, Buddhist teachers teach you about the formation of the mind from the base. It is said that the fundamental mind is our *alaya* consciousness. What is this *alaya* consciousness? It is the very deep unconscious consciousness that forms the base of your mind. This is the way we are taught, but I discovered that these teachers had concealed important points in order to make their disciples struggle by themselves to attain true knowledge. Accepting this theory that *alaya* consciousness is the base of the mind, we must realize that consciousness alone has no power to realize awareness. Consciousness needs an object, just as a mirror needs an object to be reflected upon it. Without the images reflected on a mirror, you cannot be aware of the existence of the mirror.

What are the objects that give *alaya* consciousness the ability to become aware? They are the outside objects, the so-called representations. Then, I ask, does *alaya* consciousness alone and by itself perceive the existence of representations? I answer, *alaya* consciousness must have the sense organs to perceive the images of representations. I ask, what are the sense organs of *alaya* consciousness? I answer, the sense organs of *alaya* consciousness are this physical body—these ears, eyes, and other sense organs.

When you think about *alaya* consciousness, you cannot think about it abstractly; you must think about it with the outside. When you meditate, do not close your eyes and retreat into the darkness of your mind in order to figure out what *alaya* consciousness is. This is an erroneous attitude of meditation. Keep your eyes open, and keep your ears open, and meditate upon *alaya* consciousness with its whole nature. *Alaya* consciousness always consists of the five senses and the five sense objects. Do not separate your meditation into the outside, the five senses, and *alaya* consciousness. This is wrong. You must not separate them into parts; you must meditate upon them at one time, as a whole. You, therefore, neither retreat into your own mind nor project yourself to the outside. Sit upon it, keeping all your senses open. Then you will discover the real nature of *alaya* consciousness. Remember! You misunderstand the nature of *alaya* consciousness when you cut off the outside and the five senses, returning to darkness, burying yourself, thinking that the darkness is the base of your mind. This sort of concept causes many troubles in life.

Consider the turmoil you live in by holding such a view. You destroy your house and cut off your head. Cutting off the outside world and the five senses, you try to walk only in the darkness of *alaya* consciousness and think that this is the foundation of life. As a result, you think that this world is unclean; you cover your face and your filthy body, and you say that you wish to exist only within your soul, so you do not accept food for your body, or your mind, or your five senses, and you think you are sacred.

People who have this concept of *alaya* consciousness think that it is absolute spiritual existence, that it has nothing to do with their physical body or five senses. They believe that *alaya* consciousness shines continually but that it has no form, like the sun or the sky— that it exists in some high, bright empyrean. And so their faces are turned upwards to the sky with their eyes open wide, and their hands joined together, as if bound. They live their whole life in this fashion, forgetting everything on this earth. Their feet never touch the ground; they hang from the sky. When they look down upon you, they look from the highest heaven. You will come across such people often.

Others pay no attention to existing things but place emphasis upon power alone. They think that *alaya* consciousness is power, energy. When such people rule the world, they naturally bring great disasters. You have seen examples of it. Nietzsche said that the weak must perish, and fools must be fooled—but why must they be fooled? The fools must be enlightened. Nietzsche certainly misunderstood the nature of the world and of men.

Apply these mistakes to yourself; think about your life. When you try to find the concrete base of mind, you must accept three things at the same time: the outside, your senses, and your consciousness. You cannot separate them; you must understand them in synthesis. A Buddhist must think in this concrete way. When I am asked the point of thinking this way, I answer that I do not worship heaven or hide myself in the earth. I am here, between heaven and earth, and I am the one who is really existing and who has awareness of this existence. That is my answer.

We observe the natural reaction of our mind to the outside, and we judge our actions accordingly. Otherwise we have to live like a thief in a department store. A thief *thinks* he is looking all around, but his desire makes him blind. He does not listen to his mind's reaction to his actions; his desire dominates his mind. When he tries to steal something, many eyes are upon him. Then, because he expresses his fear on his face, when things start to disappear, he will of course be caught. If you do not keep your eyes open to the outside, if you do not listen to the whispering voice within yourself and try to accept your desire, you are like a thief and must live like a thief. You cannot eliminate the outside when you think of the *alaya* consciousness.

The outside, in Buddhism, consists of the six *rajas*—the dust, filth, and things that are piled up; and the six *indriya* or roots—the five sense organs and *manas*, the mind that produces immediate reaction. (When I put my hand in the fire, for example, my natural reaction is to withdraw.) These, together with the six *vijnana*, or consciousnesses, make up the eighteen spheres of *alaya* consciousness. This is the foundation of the mind. When you study Buddhism, you will learn about these eighteen spheres. You must meditate upon them, but do not separate them—accept them as one piece. This way of thinking makes you a Buddhist. When you cut them into pieces and then try to think about them, you are a heretic, not a Buddhist.

FORMLESS MIND

ONCE WHEN THE BUDDHA WAS SOJOURNING in the quiet meditation grove of Saketa, some nuns asked him, "O Lokanatha [Lord of Worlds], we pray you to elucidate for us what fruit and what merit there will be from meditating in the 'Samadhi of Formless Mind,' in the emancipation that is neither emergence nor submergence and in the emancipation in which one lives fully in that wherein one is living?"

The Buddha replied: "O nuns, if you meditate in the 'Samadhi of Formless Mind,' in the emancipation in which one lives fully in that wherein one is living, there will be the fruit of Wisdom and the merit of Wisdom."

Formless Mind is the usual attitude of a Buddhist's mind. The Buddhist does not cherish any form, meaning thoughts, in the mind when there isn't any need to do so. This is our attitude. The untrained mind is like an alarm clock—ticktock, ticktock, with thoughts always flowing, morning and night. A man with an untrained mind has hardly the time to see anything, he is so busy with his thoughts. He doesn't know whether the day is clear or rainy. Walking home through Central Park, he doesn't notice that the moon is full, his mind is so busy. He doesn't see the beauty of the moon. He pursues mind, and mind pursues him. This is not the attitude of the Buddhist. The Buddhist knows that the mind is like the body; it needs rest. When we have used our body from morning to evening, we give it a rest. The mind also needs rest, so we cultivate the habit of resting our mind.

The mind is full of thoughts, which have form. Form means thoughts that have shape—notions about love, about fame, about money, about our squabbles with friends, about philosophy. It is our bad habit to keep this unenlightened mind, to be unable to release or emancipate ourselves from it. It is also our bad habit to think everything with reason; naturally, the conclusion is not real. After all, reason is only reason, not reality. Formless Mind means mind that has no thoughts; all thoughts are annihilated. *Samadhi* is concentration.

The question the nuns asked the Buddha is the same question many of you ask me: "What is the merit of meditating in the 'Samadhi of Formless Mind?'" You wish to know about things so you read books and think, but what is the merit, you ask, in resting with no thoughts in the brain? Will you not just go back to stupidity, to the primitive? What is the merit of going back to primal mind, Formless Mind?

Everyone asks this question. Those who take a material view of the original state of mind think it is dead, empty, like a sheet of paper, or stone or brick. They think that if the mind is not in the state of activity, it returns to the insentient state. Our view is different. We believe the mind returns to its original dynamic power. It is like the relationship between waves and the ocean. The everyday active work of the mind is analogous to the waves. When we rest in Formless Mind, the mind is like the bottomless ocean—all potentiality. It is in a state of omnipotence. It has religious meaning as well as psychological meaning. If you doubt this, try it.

But it is difficult to attain, this Formless Mind. Closing your eyes, you may think you have attained it. Perhaps you find that you are only in the midst of thoughts, not in the real state of Formless Mind at all. To reach that state you need training and many years of study in philosophy so you will not make a mistake. Of course, many people think they are in Emptiness when they are merely thinking the *term* Emptiness. It is difficult to attain this Formless Mind. If you are not studying with an authentic teacher, you run the risk of falling into pseudo-Emptiness.

Formless Mind means you are not in fixed mind. Mind is always fluctuating; it does not reside in one place. It is in a true sense "formless." Mind passes like a mirage, like images before a mirror. Knowing it is ephemeral, you do not cherish it. When you do not cherish it, you are on the ground of Formless Mind.

The dilettantes of Buddhism think that covering the eyes, the ears, and the mouth, like the three carved monkeys, is to be in Formless Mind. Their view is erroneous. It is dead Buddhism, not real Buddhism. It ruins the country, it ruins the people, it ruins the people's souls.

So what is "emergence and submergence?" What is the Buddhist view? To illustrate, you can say the human mind is like a tree; it has roots, a trunk, boughs, branches, and leaves. Our consciousness, like a tree, is in the form of a crystallization. The universe is in the form of a crystallization. Everything in nature has this form of crystallization. A tree forms according to the weather and the environment—the sun that shines, the wind that blows, and the manners of other trees standing near it; its nature is to show its own crystallization.

The human mind is exactly like a tree. According to Buddhism, there are five stages to the human mind. The bottom, or root consciousness, is divided into three parts—deepest, everlasting, and consciousness of consciousness, which is the rootless, mother consciousness. This means that we cannot, by meditation, find the bottom of this consciousness; it is fathomless.

The unconscious or semiconscious activity of the mind is like the trunk of the tree. This present consciousness reflects not only what comes in from the outside through the five senses, but also the thoughts that take place inside the mind, which are reflected upon it.

The joint of the branches is sense-perception. It is not, however, as of yet subdivided into the five branches, the five sense organs. These consciousnesses react to the outside and create many sensations—for example, the vibrations of color.

Thus our consciousness creates phenomena. This is emergence. Emergence is thought of as coming from the bottom of consciousness to the outside. Submergence is from the outside to the deepest consciousness, from the material to the everlasting consciousness.

When we analyze consciousness, we must use illustrations. The scale in music is a good abstract illustration for consciousness—do, re, mi, fa, sol, la, ti, do. Of course, music is not abstract analysis; neither is Buddhism. In meditation, when you attain emancipation from both emergence and submergence, you will be free of the "scales" of consciousness, and your consciousness will be your own. Until then, your consciousness is packaged in terms known as Buddhism. You must destroy those terms of Buddhism. Come back to your self, and meditate upon it.

Well, if your purpose is just to come back to your usual mind, why must you study, why must you practice meditation for many years? What is the merit, what is the fruit of it? This was what the nuns were wondering about. I, too, wondered about this question when I was practicing meditation, struggling so many hours in fear and agony. Then, one day, I decided: "I don't care if I ever come back. I will just stay here and meditate." Well, when I did come back, of course, I found myself in just the same place, in this world, where we are living now. We don't need more than this.

Buddhism teaches that you must live fully where you are living. You must live fully where you are. I studied Buddhism until I was forty-five years old. I entered the monastery when I was in my twenties. Now I am fifty-eight. Nothing has changed. Earth did not go up to heaven, and heaven did not come down to earth. I did not attain the state of a demi-god. I am still a human being. So, what is the merit of practicing Buddhism? Buddhism is like a toothache: when it is gone, nothing is different. Then why did I spend so much money at the dentist's?

The Buddha replied: "O nuns, if you meditate in the 'Samadhi of Formless Mind,' in the emancipation in which one lives fully in that wherein one is living, there will be the fruit of Wisdom and the merit of Wisdom."

This is the Buddha's conclusion. We attain wisdom by practicing to and fro, back and forth, through the scales of consciousness. This is the fruit of the practice of Buddhism. Our consciousness developed from the consciousness of other types of sentient beings. They have been living for millions of years in the world, but they have not attained wisdom. What is it that makes human beings different from animals? It is wisdom—self-awareness. Self-awareness is the pivot of Buddhism. We are not living in unconsciousness; we are living consciously. We are not living at the mercy of nature; we realize nature within us and use it consciously. Wisdom is nature; nature is wisdom. This wisdom is the pivot of Buddhism; we do everything with it. There is no other wisdom in human life. Wisdom is the pivot of human life.

PURE MIND

A CHILD ASKED HIS FATHER, WHO WAS ALWAYS meditating, "Father, why do you practice meditation?" The father answered, "I am trying to keep my mind pure." The child asked, "What is pure mind?" The father replied, "The mind that is like pure water—colorless, tasteless." The child said, "My teacher said that pure water has no fish in it." The father said, "He does not understand the purity of water. Water is pure no matter what is in it." The child commented, "Then, father, you do not need to practice meditation." The father said, "I practice it anyway."

To attain pure mind, you begin by keeping your mind as pure as water. You create the karma that causes you to fall into hell because of the impurities in your mind. The only reason you go to hell is that the impurities in your mind raise hell with you. The experiences you undergo cause your karma, and this karma takes place in your mind. It has no other place. The karma that you create does not stay in the sky or on the earth, or under the earth, but in your mind. Usually the working part of the mind and the stuff in it are considered together in Buddhism—mind and mind-stuff. If mind is like pure water, then mind-stuff is like ashes in it.

When the everyday mind that has mind-stuff in it relates to something else, the mind-stuff churns in the mind-water and we call it impure: "I hate her, I love him, I wish I had that . . . ." There is no hell under the earth to which you will go when you die. There is just this impure mind. This impure mind is hell.

In meditation, we keep our mind quiet and exterminate the mind-stuff to attain pure mind-power. In the morning, the mind-stuff shakes up when you go out and associate with people, but in the evening when you come home, you keep your mind quiet and let the mind-stuff settle down. When you have practiced this settling down of the mind-stuff, even though your mind is full of mind-stuff, you can feel that the nature of mind is originally pure. The great ocean that produces Mount Sumeru, the world, is not always clean and pure on the surface, but in the depths all is pure. The great man's mind is like that. Its nature is always pure. But the ordinary man's mind doesn't know that pure condition of mind.

In the daytime, the ordinary man agitates his mind. At night, even when he is sleeping, it is just the same. He dreams, hates, loves, possesses as in the daytime. There is no time that the mind settles down and there is clear water on top.

It is best to associate with people who have pure minds. If you associate with someone who has an impure mind, whatever word you say will be twisted. No word can go into his mind smoothly. Whatever you say, the impure mind will twist, while the pure-minded person will see through to your meaning immediately. You have no trouble when you associate with pure-minded people.

There are many religions in the world, but all emphasize the simple and pure mind. This is the only useful part of religion. In Christianity, in prayer, you confess everything to God and your mind becomes pure. In Buddhism, you meditate. Perhaps it will come into your mind: "He insulted me today." You shake your head and forget about it. Or: "I lost all my money today." And you shake your head and forget that, too.

MIND-STUFF

We think our Zen sect is closest to the Buddha's Buddhism. Our main emphasis is on meditation. As I am the first to bring this teaching to America, I do not put so much emphasis on meditation, but in China and Japan the monks are always meditating. It is the best method of reaching the goal of Buddhism. What is the result of meditation? What are we aiming at? To give you an answer, I must indicate the central point of Buddhism. This is not an easy task.

To practice meditation is to observe your mind-stuff and to separate it from your mind—to realize that mind-stuff is not your real mind. I have spoken many times about mind-stuff and the kinds we can observe: some kinds are like visions, dreams and notions expressed in words, and some are feelings, like obsessions. These feelings are neither visions nor notions, but impressions (*samskara*) that create the nature of the moods we put in our minds. We wish to be sad, and we are sad. This is affected, not real sadness. You can observe this at funerals: Some weep because they feel they must show grief. Many types of mind-stuff are described in Buddhist literature. You must separate these from your mind through meditation.

This was a hard task for me in the beginning, but it is now plain and simple. Subconscious mind-stuff is hard to handle because it never comes to the surface. In dreams, we reach some shallow parts of the subconscious, but the stuff there is so fine, like seeds flowing through water, that it is impossible to annihilate. In conscious states, we can annihilate much of the mind-stuff by realizing the difference between mind-stuff and the mind itself. We can think of the mind as pure fire, and the mind-stuff as snowflakes dancing in that fire. It is not easy even to make this distinction.

At first, you should try to keep the mind-stuff out of your consciousness for a given period of time, perhaps twenty minutes. You will find that the shadowy stuff will come in just as a bat flies through the evening twilight, but you must not allow your attention to follow it or you will forget that you are meditating. The arising thoughts start as smoke, but suddenly the whole city is on fire. Then you become aware and cry, "I was meditating!" This is wrestling with mind-stuff.

In American life, there is not much time for meditation. You must make time. In the morning, in the evening, even if it is only for a few minutes, take time to find the difference between mind and mind-stuff.

Of course, without mind-stuff there is no mind. Yet they are two different things. When you know this, you will touch real life, real existence itself. This is the entrance to Buddhism. Without meditation you cannot enter; it is the only method by which you can feel the real current of Buddha nature.

The Buddha emphasized meditation. Though you can understand through koans, you cannot analyze the metaphors behind these gigantic questions except through meditation. You begin meditation by watching your mind-stuff.

But do not think that meditation is Buddhism; it is only a method to open the gate.

MEDITATION

We in the East, after making some study of Western culture and civilization, have found that the only thing in the East that is not to be found in the West is what we call *samadhi*.

The European scholar Monier Williams has translated this word *samadhi* as "composing the mind, intense contemplation, perfect absorption of thought in the object of meditation." Other scholars translate it as "trance," "oblivion," or "forgetfulness." None of these definitions, however, is accurate. Temporarily, I use the word "meditation," but I must explain its significance. *Samadhi* is the transformation of one's self into that upon which one is meditating. When I transform myself into something, I forget my own existence and become this something.

Novices in Zen temples used to practice this type of meditation from a very early age. In olden days, they came to the temple when they were about eight years old and began immediately to cultivate their *samadhi*-power. Today, Zen novices do not begin their practice of meditation until about the age of sixteen, for they must first finish their primary school studies, and may prefer to finish their university courses before coming to the monastery. We call these modern monks "intelligentsia" monks; they have a knowledge of Buddhist philosophy but little *samadhi*-power.

I did not learn how to practice *samadhi* in a monastery but from my art teacher. When I was learning to paint the sea, my teacher asked his students to sketch at the seashore or copy the waves in ancient masterpieces. "Without brush or palette," he said, "go alone to the oceanside and sit down on the sand. Then practice this: Forget yourself until even your own existence is forgotten and you are entirely absorbed in the motion of the waves." We took our teacher at his word, and day after day in the summertime, we went to the seashore, to the so-called Ninety-nine-mile Beach on the Pacific Ocean, near Tokyo, and there we would stay all day long watching the waves. When we came back in the evening to our lodging houses and hotels, we felt as though we were still at the seashore listening to the pounding surf. Some young artists would stay there a week, then return to their studios in the city to seize their brushes and paint waves in the very rhythm of the sea. This is our way of art. This is also a way of *samadhi*. You transform your-self into the object you are confronting.

The Buddha founded his religion upon *samadhi*. His object of meditation was his own mind. He did not meditate upon any exter-nal object, upon thoughts or words or ideas. He meditated simply upon mind—mind from which has been extracted every thought, every image, every concept. He paid no attention either to the out-side or to the inside; he meditated upon his own mind. Perhaps we should say that mind meditated upon itself, for, in true Buddhist meditation, mind by itself is the meditator and at the same time the object of meditation.

I think the meaning of "his own mind" is not very clear to Western people. Western people think that mind, to be mind, must have something in it; if it has nothing in it, it is not mind. But con-sider the mind of an infant: it doesn't know the words papa and mama, it doesn't know its own existence, it doesn't know the out-side world; nevertheless, it has its own mind, pure and empty. I can illustrate this from the Bible. You remember Christ pointing out a child and saying that those in heaven are like that child. We can discover that mind in this world through meditation. The attain-ment of this pure and empty mind is true *samadhi*. This is Buddhism.

The Buddha practiced meditation for six years and succeeded in attaining this pure and empty mind. He did not call it God, or Mind, either. He did not call it by any name. For him, Buddhism was very simple and very pure. Buddhism is like a piece of stone, or the head of a turnip. It is pure mind. If you prefer to call it "soul," Buddhism is pure soul. Our teacher used to say to us when we practiced meditation: "Don't close your eyes; you will be bothered by your own thoughts. Don't keep your eyes open; you will be bothered by outside things. Keep your eyes partly closed and medi-tate upon your own soul." This is Buddhism.

Go to Fifth Avenue and buy any image of the Buddha. In all the images, the Buddha is represented as meditating. He is teaching his religion—his attitude of attaining enlightenment. That is Buddhism. The Buddha did not dispute like a philosopher; he practiced medi-tation. But he did not merely practice meditation; he cultivated his power of *samadhi*. He forcefully meditated upon his own soul so he could penetrate through the universe with his soul and not call it his soul any more. There is no "his soul," there is no "soul of God."

It was through *samadhi* that the Buddha transformed himself into the universe. He became the universe.

Of course, what he found was not philosophy. Philosophy is the way to find the truth by systematized logic. To practice *samadhi,* we do not need logic.

In most religions, there must be a God to worship, to whom to offer prayer. There must be a God before whom we kneel down and burn incense, to whom we offer adoration. You must look up to heaven and join your hands and call on His name. Buddhists do not do this. The Buddhist does not offer prayers, pays no adoration, does not build churches, does not have music or sing hymns. The only thing a Buddhist does is meditate. It is quite true that, from your point of view, the Buddhist has no God. We have no God, but we prove the evidence of the existence of God. We do not need to have faith in God. We *know* God. Faith? What are you talking about! Do you ask if I have faith in my own existence? I existed before I had faith in myself.

So to argue whether or not Buddhists have a God is unnecessary. It is something we have. Without struggling, we have it. Without studying, we have it. If you realize *that,* without struggle *you* can have it. If you realize the nature of this religion without reading a book, then you can have it. It is not necessary to call it Buddhism; it is not necessary to call it anything. You can have it any time, without calling it by name. Just as a long time ago we had chrysanthemums and you did not. Well, now you have chrysanthemums.

I think I have explained the nature of this religion called Buddhism. But I shall speak a little more.

Even in meditation, the Buddhist analyzes mind activity. Buddhists do not work on the analysis of mind-matter, but upon the analysis of mind activity. Dreams, for instance, are mind-matter; words and all images in the mind are mind-matter. Eddington called these "mind-stuff." The psychologist analyzes mind-stuff. Of course, the psychologist calls it "present conscious state," "subconscious state," or "unconscious state," but mostly it is mind-matter. Buddhists, however, meditate upon their own mind and eradicate all mind-stuff. That is the practice of Buddhism: to annihilate all mind-stuff and meditate upon pure mind. But you—you go back home and meditate: "I lent Mr. Jones twenty-five cents five years ago, and he hasn't paid me yet . . . . My breakfast was nice, but I've forgotten the name of the restaurant . . . ." You must eradicate all that. You try it and it's impossible. You think you will never succeed. But practice it, and one year later you will see—you will find your mind empty, not stupid but more clear. In such a way, Buddhists analyze the activity of mind.

The foundation of Buddhism is meditation. When you meditate, keep your eyes open. Your mind activity ceases; the outside becomes monotonous—all is one. You see the outside through the medium of your mind. When your mind is purified, the outside ceases to exist and you enter the world of pure mind, of soul only. Your footsteps draw near to the great cosmic mind, and you enter. Do not be afraid. You will not lose your physical body, but will return and look at your physical body and realize this body is not your own. When you experience this in meditation, it is the first step of realization in Buddhism.

THE SHAPE OF MEDITATION

To hold the physical shape of meditation, you must recognize that your spine is the central column. You must not bend your spine into the shape of a bow. Make it a straight central column, and sit as if your hands were meant to support that column. You must do this in order to meditate. You must not sit to the side on your hipbone, but straight. You must also sit very deep.

Half-close your eyes, and look to the front. Do not close your eyes during meditation because later you will find that you can be easily disturbed. Your mental shape will be disturbed. Soen Shaku, my teacher's teacher, practiced his meditation with his eyes wide open, but usually we sit with our eyes half-closed.

Such is the physical shape of zazen, which simply means "sitting meditation." In America, when we meet a friend, we shake hands; the strength is in the arm. When you walk on the street, you should put strength in the abdomen and walk straight. Some people give the impression of being intoxicated, their walk is so weak. A gentleman or lady must cultivate dignity. Therefore, you must practice the shape of meditation whenever you have time. People who cannot keep this shape are very undignified. They come to a house as a guest and very soon are leaning back with their feet up on a chair. Such slouching is undignified. Naturally, there are formal, semiformal, and informal attitudes; but even the so-called informal has a kind of formality.

When you study a sport, the teacher teaches you the shape of your body. In Japan, we study fencing and judo. The teacher always teaches the physical shape. In Zen temples, novices must practice keeping this shape before they study koans. I might add that it is not good to look from the corner of the eyes. I once met a Zen master in Japan who was like a wild boar when he looked at you. He never turned his head or moved his eyes to look at something. When he turned, he moved from the waist, turning his whole upper body.

It is equally important to keep the shape of the mind. In order to keep the shape of the mind, you must keep the shape of the body. If you keep the body straight, the shape of the mind will be straight.

It is easy to keep the shape of the body, but keeping the shape of the mind is not so easy.

To explain "keeping the shape of the mind," I will use the five *skandhas,* or shadows of the mind. *Rupa skandha* is all objective existence. According to the five *skandhas* theory, Buddha thought of our physical body as a state of mind. When you move your body, you are expressing your mental body with your physical body. Keep your physical body in shape.

After *rupa skandha,* the second *skandha* is *vedana,* the sense organs. All the sense organs must be kept in shape. To do this I have always personally concentrated in the ear, hearing all sounds at once and refusing none. In quietude, everyone is disturbed when sounds come from the outside, from the elevated trains, horns, and the like. When we are disturbed, we cannot meditate. We are disturbed because we are refusing those sounds entrance. We do not intentionally receive such sounds, but we must make complete unity with them. When I was working under the Third Avenue El, it was so noisy I could not hear my own thoughts. I decided to accept this noise without refusing it, and it wasn't noisy anymore. Of course, it wasn't so comfortable, but I was not disturbed. When I am giving a lecture and the musician next door plays, I accept it as if I were paying him; then he doesn't annoy me. After all, there is nothing to meditate upon.

The third *skandha* is *samjna.* This is the main point of the training, the head of the monkey that must be trained in zazen. You cannot refuse thoughts that rise to the shelf of the mind like air bubbles—from unconsciousness and semiconsciousness to consciousness. Nevertheless, such bubbles must be burst before they reach the highest state. Let these thoughts come—cigarettes, music, beefsteak, a glass of water. You cannot refuse them, but you must not entertain any of them. Let them come; let them go. Your mind must be like a mirror, reflecting but never holding what it reflects. Thoughts are independent existences. Subjective thoughts belong to you, but objective thoughts belong to the outside. If you entertain them subjectively, your thoughts will disturb the shape of your mind.

The fourth *skandha* is *samskara.* The thoughts that we have just discussed—about cigarettes and the like—have shape or form. Words are the symbols of thoughts. When I say "water," the word is the symbol of the thoughts connected with water. But this is not *samskara*. *Samskara* has no words and no figures. *Samskara* is feeling. It is mood. It is emotion. Essentially, it is emotion. It is always in motion like water, air, or fire. When *samskara* moves, you feel that emotion, or mood of mind. Such experiences cannot be completely expressed in words. This is the realm of the poet, who tries to put emotion into words and always feels more than can possibly be written down. *Samskara* is a very big world. All things in the sleeping state are in *samskara*. Trees and animals are in it. Every tree and animal also has its characteristic emotion. To keep the shape of your mind, you must keep your mood and your emotion. When you kill or lie to yourself, you cannot do it.

The root, ground, or foundation is consciousness—*vijnana*, the fifth *skandha*. It is bottomless. Do not think it has a bottom. Do not ever think: "That is the bottom. There is God!" The feeling of God is bottomless. There is nothing in the bottom of the mind. This bottomless mind itself is a mirror, receiving impressions of mood and thoughts and of the outside. Keep your mind in shape as you meditate on thoughts, moods, and emotions. Then you can create your actions from the bottom of your mind.

I am very lazy, but I trained for a long time to keep my mind in shape. When I came to America, I saw that people here have no training in form or shape, for their expression is non-formal. Americans have their own shape, but it is not a cultured shape. When you do not keep control, your mind is out of shape, non-formal.

When you enter the Zen room, try to keep your body and mind in shape. The Zen room is a battlefield. Be trained in zazen! That is your basic training, your boot camp. It is also the training for daily life. Zen is a very practical religion.

MOTIONLESS MIND

Quiescence of mind is just sitting quietly, tranquilly connecting to the great mind, the mind of the universe. It is motionless mind, the mind of the great ox, the great cow, the great elephant—not the mind of a little dog or a chattering human being.

In meditation, make the mind as motionless as a mountain. To practice this, you must have faith that you are going back to the original mind of the great universe, original nature. You must know that you are one with the universe. This idea handled mentally prevents you from entering the mind of the universe. Do not make the mistake of trying to grasp it with your brain. Grasp it with integral existence, with your whole nature. Do not think, using the mind.

Your attitude toward a saint will be the same as that toward a criminal. When you meet a saint, you will not smile, and when you meet a criminal, you will not frown. You will communicate with everyone as with yourself. You do not need to take any special attitude toward anyone you confront. This is the usual attitude of Zen students. Do not feel that you must maintain your dignity, or impress your greatness upon anyone. Meet everyone just as you would meet the soul of the universe.

If you become one with nature, you do not need to flatter the powerful or scorn the weak. With your quiescence, you will meet the other's quiescence. This is the real meaning of democracy. It was the attitude of Lincoln. It is being the same with a steelworker as with a famous philosopher.

Many students think that quiescence is motionlessness of the physical body. What is the position of meditation? People pay fifty dollars for a train ticket to come here and ask me how to hold the spine, how to close the eyes, how to breathe, how to count the breaths, how to take in the air through the nostrils. Physical posture is important, of course, but the mental attitude of meditation is more important. They do not ask questions about that. They ask how to breathe through the nose—as though it were something mysterious.

The Zen student meets others as an ox meets a chicken. Of course, when you practice meditation for a long time, you will find this out naturally. When you cultivate your own position of mind, you will find out how to adapt yourself to each person you meet, according to his or her nature and state of mind. Practice meditation and mind your own business. If you talk about whether others are right or wrong, you are violating the law of your own intrinsic nature.

Your mind should be as big as the sky, not as small as the water in a glass. It should be as deep as the ocean, with only the waves on the surface fluctuating. The water at the bottom of the sea is eternally quiet. You will talk and smile, but the bottom of your mind will be empty and still, reaching to the empty universe.

In ancient days, a Chinese novelist wrote: "No one can understand a woman's mind, because it is empty." But I think that man's mind is also empty—as empty as the sky.

If there is anything in your mind, it is ego. When you are man made by man and not by God, you are violating the law of intrinsic nature.

If you adhere to pureness of mind, you are practicing what is called "fox meditation." The dilettante, like the fox in a cave, meditates in darkness. Many people make this mistake. I saw a man cover his face with his cap. "Why?" I asked him. "Because I don't want to see the ugly world." Keep your eyes open. What is wrong with the outside world, the world of the four elements—earth, water, fire, and air? That which is wrong in the world is the human mind. So don't close your eyes, keep them half-open. At the beginning, perhaps, it is easier to keep the eyes closed, but this is not permitted for more than half a year to ten months. Direct the eyeballs to the left or right, as in the statue of the Buddha, not looking straight in front, for that makes the eyes cross. This is the true attitude of meditation.

Do not think anything about pureness of mind. When you try to keep your mind empty, you think this is pureness of mind, but it is dilettante meditation.

Real meditators take no such attitude. Their minds are like the calm moon in the empty sky. Clouds, stars, wind, spring, summer, autumn, and winter come and go, but the quiet moon in the sky does not move. It is the driven clouds that move. All will go through your brain and heart, will be reflected, but your mind will not go with it. You must practice meditation for a long time to realize this. If you adhere to each phenomenon that comes to mind, that adherence becomes an obstruction to the Way, the Law of the universe.

In meditation, the mind extends endlessly to east, west, north, and south; the center pervades throughout the universe. The spatial, three-dimensional mind is molded in such a way, but in meditation the mind is also molded in duration, which is a wonderful thing. This duration is not a straight line, but is expanding. Perhaps you could call it the fourth dimension. The Oriental does not use these words, but certainly in meditation we can experience that fourth-dimensional space.

You are the master in all circumstances. You are not sitting upon your chair but on top of the universe. There are many words that describe this: You are sitting on top of the universal sun, the Absolute, Vairochana Buddha. This earth, not the universe, has day and night. The universe of meditation, also, has neither day nor night because you are sitting on top of the universal sun. But don't take this literally, and don't dramatize yourself. Just sit calmly.

When you finally behold the quiescence of your own mind, or nature, within yourself, it is not as easy to understand. But when you have passed the first koan—"Before father and mother, what were you?"—and you reach your original nature, there is neither inside nor outside, neither time nor space, neither spirit nor matter. Then there is no word to think, no silence to keep, no sound to refuse to hear. You lose the bottom of your mind and go back to universal nature. From the top of your head to the tip of your toes, you will realize your original nature. And when you behold IT—not thinking, not talking about it—this is called Zen. The English word "meditation" is so small that it does not cover the true attitude called Zen.

NOTING

The sutras and the Agamas mention various methods of counting the breaths in meditation. It is best to use a simple method. Do not pay attention to the amateurs who count in-breathing through the right nostril and out-breathing through the left nostril. They may have read some meditation guide and developed their own method without an experienced teacher. You must simply know when you are inhaling and when you are exhaling.

You count in order to keep your awareness concentrated. This awareness is a key with which you may attain enlightenment. The goal of meditation is to wake you up. Otherwise, you could meditate for a hundred years to no avail.

Carefully watch the thoughts that haunt your mind. In the daytime these appear as daydreams; at night they are dreams. You must watch your thoughts as a cat watches a mouse, or as a guard watches for a burglar. Counting helps to eliminate them. It is best, in meditation, to count in simple numbers—one to ten for example, and no more than fifty. When you count into the hundreds, your meditation becomes a dream.

When you are meditating, you must sort out your thoughts. What kinds of thoughts enter your mind? Do they relate to your koans or to other thoughts? You must also watch the irregular coming of thoughts—can you count their four phases (of birth, being, decay, and death)? When you are awake, the thoughts probably stay only a little while, but when you are sleepy—no matter how you clear your mind—you cannot keep the thoughts from coming in. However, you need not entertain these thoughts. This is as though you are counting them one by one.

In your meditation, do not let any thought pass without stamping it! Be like an immigration officer. One, two, three. It is said of a haunting ghost that if you call its name, it disappears. So it is with thoughts. They vanish when you become aware of them. It is something like the work of the psychologists today, who must know what thoughts are "eating" their patients. Only then can the thoughts be named.

With tranquil awareness, the meditator observes thoughts one by one as they pass through the mind. This can be done by counting breaths. It can be understood as "rhythm," so counting is not necessary. What is necessary is to "note" the action that you are performing. When you breathe rhythmically, it has nothing to do with counting in numbers. With care, your mind will follow the breath.

Now, to use this awakened awareness, keep note of your thoughts coming in and going out. When you have practiced this for a long time, you will realize that you are in the state of *dhyana* (meditation). It is like practicing the piano—at first, you are paying attention to your practice, but after a while it is as if another person is playing. You are not doing it. Does a skillful rider bump against the horse? No. Upon the horse is no rider, and beneath the rider is no horse—they are one. The practice of *dhyana,* or "noting", is like this.

Thus, your power of awareness will gradually increase. You will be aware of hundreds and thousands of worlds as you behold the objects of your everyday world. A single drop of rain, a million worlds! The whole universe appears before you—as this world. It comes, it stays. It decays and goes. It appears as Emptiness, then as Reality. But suddenly, you will realize that *all* is your own consciousness. In one observation, all phenomena lie before you. If you really attain this state, you have attained buddhahood.

In this power of awareness, as it increases, you can attain many things. To train your awareness, you must keep sharpening it, putting it back into the furnace. In English, this awareness is called the sixth sense.

When you practice meditation and *sanzen,* the answer to your koan will arise from this aspect of your mind. You must not think about it—it is the answer that springs into your mind that you must trust. It is an instantaneous decision.

We all have this power of quick decision, instinctively, but we have spoiled it. It is called *prajna* (intuitive wisdom). Only a teacher can test and know if a student has attained this. In this respect, Zen is different from all other religions.

Do not forget these words. Note them. It's how you increase your own wisdom. One day you will say: "Twenty years ago Sokei-an said this. Now I have come to it."

RUNNING WATER

ONE DAY THE BUDDHA TOLD HIS DISCIPLES: "Your mind is like running water. Trees and rootless weeds flow along with it. This tree, as it floats along, pays no attention to the trees flowing beside it, nor do those other trees pay any attention to this tree. The one ahead does not notice the one behind, nor does the one behind recognize the one ahead. Your mind is exactly like this. This mind-stuff and that mind-stuff—all the bits of debris that are floating on the water of pure soul—do not recognize each other. One flows and the other follows. The one that precedes does not know the follower, nor does the follower know the one that precedes. One after another, they flow with the water of pure soul. On the earth, under heaven, there is no place you can call your own; there is no rest and no joy through countless incarnations. If a body has no eye, it does not know where it is going. If a mind has no eye, it does not know the direction in which it is running."

The Buddha is talking about his enlightenment. He is trying to tell you that your mind must have an eye. If you observe your mind from morning to evening, you can see it is like a river in flood. You are writing a letter—you write about four lines, then you go to the kitchen and cut up a few potatoes, go back to the letter and write a few more lines; then you want a cigarette, but you can't find any, so you go to the store; then you go to a movie—your mind is flowing without uniformity. Why? Because it has no center. There is no eye in it.

A vegetable has no eye. A tree has no eye. They feel unconsciously. Great Nature, instinct, does the work. For instance, there are male and female gingko trees, but they are in a helpless situation, for they have no sight. The seed of the male tree must be carried by the wind for twenty miles through the sky to reach the female tree where the flower catches it and conceives. It's casual because there is no eye.

Developed animals have eyes and perhaps some ideas, though many of the lower species have only a sense of touch not much better than that of weeds, so they do not remember as we do.

When they hunt for food it is by instinct—it's casual, a lucky strike. They do not know how to sow seed or grow food. They have no goals. The animal mind depends totally upon instinct, the bosom of nature. How poor they seem! Some human beings are in that class. But a human being has a mind. Wonderful, isn't it, that we have this mind, that we think this and that, all day, all year, all our life long?

Some human beings think the way a spider spins a web. They cannot find the center of their thoughts. They cannot concentrate their thought to one spot. Their thoughts are like the seeds of the gingko tree floating in the air. They are going every which way because they have no concentrative ability. They cannot gather the mind nor govern it, nor can they observe it from a higher step. They are blind because they have no eye in their minds.

The body of the human being is not flesh; it is mind. This flesh is the body of the animal, the body of the gingko tree. The blossom is the tree's eye. This physical eye is our blossom. The human being, a strange being, is living in the mind. Have you ever observed the body of mind? Perhaps never. If I say to you the "body of mind," what do you think of? The body of mind is not unlike a jellyfish. It expands, contracts, grows, circles, diverges, converges. It has its own peculiar existence. Of course, the animal body has sex, but the human body, the body of mind, has no sex. The body of mind is like an amoeba. It divides to beget more existences. During the moment when I am talking and you are listening, here at this moment, there is just one united body of mind, united. Then it divides and its offspring scatter, joining one to the other; and those unite to beget more. You must look at the human being from a higher viewpoint. It lives in the animal body but it takes an independent attitude.

The eye of the mind! If I give you the koan "Before father and mother, what was your original aspect?" you cannot answer because this body-mind cannot find its eye. Why? Because it never comes to its center, the eye of the mind. Foolish, isn't it? You start to spin your web—thinking, thinking, thinking, and what have you got really? Nothing.

We do not care for those trees or weeds that flow in the water of the mind. The existence of our mind depends on that pure water of mind flowing without weeds and trees, not on the debris. Before your mother and father, is there mind-stuff to talk about? Before creation, is there any mind-stuff to talk about? There is no past, present, no such words. There is no way to think about it. Stop that spinning. Come back to your real existence, find your eye of mind.

When the Buddha said, "Attain buddhahood," he meant open your own eye of mind. The eye of mind is the flower of the universe. The lotus bud of your mind will open, and you will find the eye in the center of the flower of the universe. By opening the eye of the mind, Buddha said, you will understand the benevolence of your teacher.

But you come to my room and speak. If I were permitted, I would give you thirty blows. Without a teacher, you can occasionally find the eye of the mind, but you do not believe it. So the teacher proves it for you. If you are with your teacher, the Buddha said, you will depend on your teacher's instructions. If you are far away, you will think of his words. When you open the eye of your mind, you will have pity on those who are blind, and you will laugh at the six ways—the lower states of hell, hungry ghosts, and animals, and the higher states of humans, angry demons, and gods.

In hell, you will find that you are not in agony. When you see the hungry demons who never find food, the animals who must labor always, and the angry spirits and gods who dwell in your mind *with* the eye of mind, none of them will bother you; you will find your own world. You will look at your mind, animal, and vegetable body, and locate yourself in the universe. You will find freedom there.

MINDLESSNESS

In anxiety and agony, the Buddhist takes refuge in the Buddha's teaching. In sickness, the Buddhist takes the view that the physical body is like a bubble, like morning dew in the garden that the sun will soon melt away. It is not true existence. It is temporal existence that has emerged from Emptiness and will submerge into Emptiness. Knowing this, the dying Buddhist closes his eyes, taking refuge in Emptiness.

When I was at the battlefront and under fire, during the Russo-Japanese War, I often thought of this teaching: "My existence is like the lightning that flashes through the dark air. My life is so short, it is like a dream. When I draw my last breath, I will return to the original Emptiness, the original substance that timelessly exists. Why should I be afraid?" And I did not hesitate to walk into the shower of fire.

Buddhism gives us great strength at the end of life, or in a predicament, but it is even more wonderful to take refuge in Mindlessness than in Emptiness. We suffer most in our minds. Almost every day, every moment, our minds torture us. Many times I hate my mind.

Our wooden fish drum is the symbol of Mindlessness, for we think the fish has sense-perceptions but no mind. Animals have minds, but fish do not, we say. Fish are not blind to what happens outside, but they respond mindlessly. When we beat upon our wooden drum, it too responds mindlessly.

Zen training saves us from being enslaved by our mind, emancipates us from the torture of the mind. We practice many, many years to reach the mindless attitude. We think of our mind as a cloud passing through the sky over the moon. It looks as if the moon is sailing, but it is actually the cloud sailing by. When we are suffering from our mind, we think our soul is suffering. But sickness is not soul, sickness is mind, mind passing over the surface of the soul. We think the soul is sick, but the soul does not suffer. If we stop the suffering of our mind, the illness will be removed.

Many stories of Japanese heroes concern Mindlessness. One warrior who had lost a battle decided to commit suicide. With the enemy surrounding him, he said, "I wish to write a letter to my mother. Please wait." When the letter was finished, he called an attendant. "Send this." Then he cut his throat. There was no excitement; not because he was cold-blooded, but because he was mindless. He did this as I would drink a glass of water. He was like the fish with five senses and a soul, but no mind.

When I am troubled, I wonder why; then I remember it is my mind, and I do not squeeze my face into an uncomfortable expression. I have a friend who squeezes his face as his cigarette grows shorter. I thought it was because he smoked so much; then I noticed that he squeezes his face even when he is not smoking, so I realized it was not his cigarette, it was his mind.

When I first came to this country, I noticed that many of the young men walking on the street had disdainful looks on their faces. They must hate everyone. They look at the world as though it were dirty. This is mind suffering.

Buddhists have defined fifty-three kinds of minds—jealous, malicious, egotistic, mocking, foolish, cruel, and so on. These minds are always being carried on the surface of our soul. We look at the world through these minds. No wonder the world appears so distorted.

Because my mind was tortured, I decided to eradicate it and become mindless. Zen meditation is the practice of becoming mindless. When you meditate, mind comes up like a bubble from the bottom of a bottle. It struggles to the surface and disappears. If you watch your thoughts, you will see them going round and round in a crazy way. In meditation, we practice stopping that mind entirely. This practice will simplify your life and bring you comfort.

Zen meditation is not to meditate *on* something, but to handle the mind as though it doesn't belong to you. Of course, it sounds strange to say that you will become mindless, but it is better than being sick-minded. We say your mind must become pure and transparent. Get rid of your useless mind. Throw it away and become mindless.

PRAYER

Christianity emphasizes offering prayer to God. What is prayer to the Buddhist? How do Buddhists pray?

Heavenly desire is prayer. Earthly prayer comes from selfish desire. But when we pray for peace and happiness for all sentient beings, desire and prayer are one, and this desire is the foundation of our life. Without desire, earthly life has no meaning; prayer is the foundation of our religious life.

Our first real prayer is to cut off our selfish nature. Today is the result of yesterday's prayer, and today is the cause of tomorrow's prayer. We offer our prayer to the future, and that prayer is heard and answered today. Praying that all prayer will be heard and answered, we continue the great prayer.

But now we must ask: To whom do we pray, to whom do we offer our prayer? Of course, the answer is clear. It should not be necessary to speak of it, but I will mention some things to be avoided, some unnecessary things that people do because they do not know true prayer.

If you go to Japan or China, you will see men and women kneeling down before an image of the Buddha or a *bodhisattva* (an enlightened being), praying on behalf of a sick mother or a dying father. Some offer prayer to Avalokiteshvara, the Bodhisattva of Mercy.

One of my cousins offered prayers every morning to Avalokiteshvara while beating on the wooden fish drum. She never stopped, no matter what happened. On the day of the big earthquake, she put her large image of Avalokiteshvara on her back and tried to run through the great conflagration raging through Tokyo. Everyone cried out to her, "Throw it away!" but she refused. A friend found her body with the image still on her back. He spoke of her faith in Avalokiteshvara: "Well, she is certainly in heaven." I could not say a word, but I pitied her, thinking, "This is not real prayer." Her eagerness was pathetic; she was stupid.

Of course, you might not carry an image of Avalokiteshvara on your back. But might you not carry some mental image in your mind, which you would not give up, even when confronting death? It is the same, this attachment to a mental conception that you can-

71

not abandon, while dying in a mental conflagration. You laugh at my cousin, and I laugh at you. She was uneducated, so she carried a material object; you are educated, but you carry mental objects. If there is any subjective notion in your mind, you are not praying a true prayer. The true prayer is: "I will not have any notion in my mind, I will not attach to any notion. My mind is one pure existence of Emptiness." Emptiness means pure existence that has no notion in it—like pure water.

If you go to Fifth Avenue to buy a crystal ball, you will look to see if there are any air bubbles in it; if so, it is an imitation. A real crystal ball has nothing in it. Our conception of Emptiness is like a crystal ball—its emptiness is not a void. This is the main point of Buddhism. If nature were a void, there would be no power, no source.

We cannot find anything outside the universe. The universe is not a void, it is something. Observing it from the original angle, we call it Emptiness. Seeing it in our mind, it is like the waves of the ocean, changing at every moment. We see the water as waves, as the body of the ocean, but at the bottom there are no waves, there is stillness. We call it Emptiness, *sunyata*. We enter this stillness through meditation, and we see through that body of mind, of soul, just as we see through the body of the ocean to the bottom. This is true prayer. By holding that prayer, we drop off all agonies, all disturbances, all unnecessary desires, and we know the Reality that is the true life of the human being. We are not living in phenomena, or in mind-stuff. To realize this life is Reality itself. Keeping this prayer, we know the laws of heaven, earth, and man. This clear understanding today will bring tomorrow's peace.

Those who dream are not praying. We must know how to pray the true prayer, must realize that life is Reality. This is the main principle of Buddhism. There is just one fundamental method. Many sects alter the method, but they eventually fall into this three-fold method. If you really grasp this three-fold way, then living in America is the same as listening to the words of the Buddha directly from his lips.

From the temporary world, we enter Emptiness. The first stage is to leave the unreal. What is the unreal? Color, sound, smell, touch, and taste are unreal—they have no real value. I am sure you are not so ignorant as to believe that color—red, blue, yellow—is an object. Color is vibration.

So we enter into oneness, the clear, pure oneness of Emptiness. Using science, you analyze objective existence and find the monad, the electron, the proton. But yesterday's science is gone now. So we analyze our mental situation, clear it out. By contemplation we enter into calm meditation. This is one angle.

The second angle is that from this calm Emptiness, we observe the surface of the waves. We see the sky, the hurricane—all is a phantom, a dream, not true life. Nothing exists objectively, all exists subjectively, a creation of our deepest consciousness, the *alaya* consciousness, the manifestation of Emptiness. To see the manifestation as electron and proton is not seeing true form, but the organization of form. Therefore, it is not true observation.

The first angle is stopping motion. From the second angle, we observe everything as a dream, looking at it from the state of Emptiness. From this aspect, we fold our arms and observe the world: everything is going and coming, the flowers of spring and the leaves of autumn. "Alas, they fade" is poetic, but not true observation.

The third angle is true observation. Why analyze? Why speak of electrons and protons? Why make the mind calm and enter into Emptiness? All this is unnecessary—this is not phenomena, nor is it Emptiness. It is not necessary to wipe out the waves; as long as the ocean exists, there will be waves. We must observe both at once. Then we realize the original aspect. Avoiding all the factitious analysis and meditation, we can observe it directly as it is: it is existing, it has always existed, and will always exist. It is neither phenomena nor noumena. Avoiding all mind activities, we observe everything exactly as it is. Then we have found the true ground of our life. This is true observation.

So we have three views of life and Reality: life is phenomena; life is noumena; wipe out both views and come to Reality. So we wipe out the outer dream, wipe out the inner dream, and come to Mind itself. Then we live our daily life, which is, in itself, the power, the Reality.

In Zen practice we have these three terms for the three stages: *samatha*—motionlessness; *samapatti*—observation from stillness; *dhyana*—no distinction between noumena and phenomena.

At every moment you must concentrate into what you are doing. When all doubt is resolved, you can take the hand of Reality and live in Wisdom.

THE HARMFUL VIEW OF EMPTINESS

From ancient days, Buddhist teachers have transmitted the Dharma to their followers and have preached to their disciples as they thought. Those ancient teachers left their teachings in the form of scrolls and books for the sake of their disciples and followers before they went away from this world.

I have attained some enlightenment by following my teacher, who transmitted his Zen to me. Every day, from morning to evening, I think about many things in Buddhism to decide my questions. Besides talking about Zen, I talk about this thinking. For a long time I have been wanting to tell you about a very important view in Buddhism, so that you will not misunderstand Buddhism in the future. I hope Buddhism will be spread gradually in the Western hemisphere in order to create mutual understanding between East and West. Those who follow me sincerely must spread Buddhism in the West, following my method of transmitting Zen separate from these sermons, and talking about Buddhism as I do according to authentic scriptures.

The important view I am going to speak about now is the so-called "harmful view of Emptiness." You must tell future audiences about this.

The harmful view of Emptiness is not a new view in Buddhism. It is a very, very old view. In India, such a view has been dominant at times—of course, among those outside of Buddhism. The Buddha talked about it many times, warning his disciples not to fall into that pit.

What is the harmful view of Emptiness? Those who do not believe in the law of causation adhere to this view of Emptiness. The Buddha said in a sutra contained in the *Abhidharma* [a collection of discourses on metaphysics and doctrines]: "What is this wrong view of Emptiness? If you think that all is empty, that there is neither this nor that, this is called the 'wrong view of Emptiness.'"

Those who have a wrong view of Emptiness usually think that there is neither this (existence) nor that (non-existence), that originally there is nothing at all in the universe. You often hear this. I have said many times that, in the end, there is neither this nor that; and those who attach themselves to their own view of Emptiness use my words to try to prove their view. I can definitely feel when someone holds that view; it is immediately evident to my feeling that the view of Emptiness has been misunderstood. Such a person holds a materialistic view of Emptiness, taking the words "neither this nor that" to mean that there is nothing in the universe, and that there is not any universe either. Without reasoning, you can see that this view is entirely erroneous. Such people have never experienced any meditation or Zen attainment. They merely follow the words "there is neither existence nor non-existence." They think that in the beginning of the universe there was nothing at all. So this existence is nothing either. By some delusion, we see these things around us, but what we see is only a mirage. There was no cause, and there will be no effect, so we do not need to bother with any law at all. The laws of this world have no basis, so we are not obliged to accept any law from others; nor do we need to follow any agreement ourselves. We Buddhists say that such a view is a "harmful view." Those who hold it destroy everything precious in human life. They are intoxicated.

Some Mahayanists, too, take such a view. They study Mahayana Buddhism, and, taking an "empty" view of Mahayana, brush all existing laws aside. Many times my friends have come to me and said: "Well, I follow Buddhism because Buddhism speaks about Emptiness, and Buddhists believe in annihilation. All these existing things are just some mechanism erroneously created by our senses. When you wake up, you will realize all is empty." Such a person must practice zazen and attain the knowledge of Zen.

In the old days of theoretical meditation, the meditator would meditate upon the scales in *rupadhatu,* the world of the senses. There are eighteen different scales upon which the meditator meditates. You begin by meditating upon this existing appearance. Of course, from the beginning, in authentic meditation, there is nothing that you have to embrace in your mind. You ask: "Shall I meditate upon a word or subject?" I answer: "You do not need to meditate on any word or subject, any diagram or thought." This is not necessary. This has never been Buddhist meditation. Meditation upon existing phenomena is not like this.

For instance, you go to Riverside Drive and sit on a bench on this side of the river and look at New Jersey. You see New Jersey on the other side. You sit on your bench and observe it. Slowly your thoughts go away, until nothing is left in your mind. When you are entirely absorbed in the view of New Jersey, *in Zen,* that moment is called *samadhi.* In *samadhi,* you observe New Jersey from this side of the river. That is the way meditation begins.

Or perhaps, you hear the sound of the gong with your mind trained in *samadhi.* At midnight, in the quiet temple, when you are meditating alone in the darkness, you hear the sound of the gong creeping into the meditation hall: "Gong . . . Gong . . ." and again, "Gong!" This is called *samadhi* in the gong.

Slowly you leave color and sound and retreat into the state of mind-by-itself. Yet, you will still observe the fragments of the outside, which have filtered through into your mind, and remain in your subconscious. They appear before your mind like gossamer in a summer field. Slowly you enter the highest state of *rupadhatu,* the world of sense. After which, your meditation will slowly ascend to *arupadhatu,* the state of pure mind only. First there is pure space, next pure consciousness, then you go into pure Emptiness.

Before the Buddha had experienced all these states and had reached his highest empty state, the teachers of that time taught that the emptiness of *arupadhatu* was the highest state obtainable. Even in this empty state of *arupadhatu,* there is no harmfulness. *Arupadhatu* is pure mind, empty mind. But when this mind comes back to this world, it comes back according to the law of this world, the law of the senses, the law of the body. The previous Buddhas too—that is, the Buddhas before Shakyamuni—had an "empty view," but it was entirely different from the harmful view of Emptiness.

In the Buddha's time there were a number of famous heretics and six different heretical teachings. Among the heretics, Purana Kashyapa was the one who had this harmful view of Emptiness. He thought that when you do good things in this world there will be no good result; there is no reward for your good deeds. If you do bad things, in the future there will be no bad result; you need never receive punishment, for no one will punish you. From the beginning, all *dharmas* are empty-natured. Therefore, between parent and child, between master and subject, there is no morality or filial piety. That was his view. Thinking that this is the Buddhist's view, people say that to believe in Emptiness is very bad, for those who believe in Emptiness think they can do everything they want to, and their minds become poisoned.

In my teaching of Buddhism or Zen, students enter slowly into

Zen, slowly into Emptiness. If someone with this wrong understanding tells them it is bad to believe in Emptiness, they may become confused. For this reason you must understand this Emptiness quite deeply.

Usually people have one of two views of Emptiness. Some think that everything exists forever: mountains exist as mountains; rivers exist as rivers; Mr. Sasaki's soul exists as it is and never changes; Mr. So-and-so's soul exists forever and will never perish. Others have this harmful view: There is nothing at all, nothing exists. You appear here like an air bubble and "Psst!"—no more! Those who hold this harmful view never believe in consciousness and the many different stages of consciousness. We are living here in these surroundings in a conscious state, and when our consciousness changes, we shall be in different surroundings. Those with the harmful view do not believe this.

I feel very sorry for those who fall into this harmful view of Emptiness and never come out of it. The Buddha said that anyone who falls into this harmful view can never be saved. So the Buddhist teaches the true view of Emptiness very carefully, never using the word emptiness to teach it, for the word emptiness is a poisonous word. If you fall into that view, you must ask the teacher. Do not decide by yourself and make your own conclusions about Buddhism. Ask the teacher.

In volume twenty of the *Ekottarika-agama* there is a story about the Buddha's true view of Emptiness. There was a monk whose name was Mrigasirsa. He was a Brahman in the beginning. His occupation was telling people where their beloved ones had gone by examining their skulls. "After his death, he went to such-and-such a heaven or hell," he would say. Or: "This is the skull of a woman. She died of such-and-such an illness; her bones were eaten by acid and her viscera dissolved into water. After her death, she fell down to hell." In such a way, Mriga talked about people's fortunes. He met the Buddha and tried to contest his knowledge against the Buddha's. The Buddha took in his hand the skull of the monk Udayana, who had died at the foot of the Gandhamadana Mountains in the Nirvana where nothing is left behind. That was his attainment while living. The Buddha showed his skull to Mriga, saying, "Now, tell me, where has he gone?" The Brahman took the skull and looked it all over but could not find where Udayana had gone. He said: "He has gone into Absolute Emptiness." Then the

Buddha said: "The monk Udayana is living in the state where there is neither end nor beginning, neither life nor death; for him there is no place to go." That was the Buddha's answer. In one word, the Buddha's Emptiness was mental emptiness, empty mind, because his whole universe is Mind itself—there is no place outside Mind.

Of course, there are many places outside the human mind, but there is no place outside this Great Mind. When you have faith in this great and true Empty Mind, you will never fall into the materialistic view of Emptiness. I hope you will remember this sermon, and when anyone tells you that Buddhists believe in Emptiness and that therefore they do not observe any morality, or any law, you will say that such a view is erroneous.

THE WORLD OF BOUNDLESS LIGHT

A story is told of a queen of India who, through no fault of her own, was confined in a dungeon with no hope of escape. Shakyamuni Buddha sent Ananda to tell her that she could emancipate herself by meditation. At any moment, her soul could step out of her body and take refuge in the boundless light of the universe. This is the origin of the Amida sect. "Amida" means endless light. We are just sparks of this light; each of us will return to it.

It would be wonderful if we could do this right now—just step out of our skins! We all wish to get out, as though we were imprisoned in a dungeon. But we cannot succeed while we are searching for something outside.

There is just one way to step out at any time. Shakyamuni Buddha found that way and taught it to us. It is as though you were an orange with one seed in the center. You must always come back to that seed, and from there, you can step out, because that centermost spot is the only spot that speaks loudly about the truth of the universe. Can you find that center in yourself? You have no seed that is tangible, but certainly you have a center in yourself. Where is it? If you try to find it, you will search in vain; but if you do not try, it is there like a moonprint in the water. You cannot grasp it— do not touch it! The moon is floating on the surface of the waves. If you abandon all your attention toward anything, you will come into that center. What is it? You think, see, hear, smell, touch, taste; you are conscious of yourself.

Where is the center? Everyone says consciousness is the center, but do not make this mistake! Who knows that your consciousness is reflecting all phenomena? Who knows that consciousness? Can consciousness know itself, or does something else know? There is something deeper in you that knows that the eye reflects. In meditation, you will know that there is a center, all shadows reflecting upon it. Imagine a crystal ball inside you and that the knowledge is held in its center. But this knower cannot be caught, because the knower is the catcher—only the knower knows its knowing! It is like standing upon a pinpoint; you cannot move from this centermost focus of yourself. This point is the one seed in the orange, and you are within the seed. The only way to step out is from there.

There is nothing more to say about this; all that is left is the practice. I cannot explain it any deeper than this. So step back into that center, and step out. But do not have any conception about standing in the center of light and soaring out like a bird.

It is not easy to understand the real meaning of boundless light, but there is a way to reach it. You can step into your innermost spark, and with that spark, you can annihilate yourself. When you prove what it is by yourself, you will find it entirely different from your previous conceptions. No one can teach you to swim on the floor—you must learn in the water. So practice this in meditation.

THE *SAMADHI* OF FIRE

We do not need beautiful scenery around us

to practice Zen meditation.

When we quench our mind,

we feel cool—

Even in the flame of fire.

This is a famous Zen poem. When we meditate in the heat of summer, we always recall this poem. Zen students take refuge in meditation in all circumstances: when we are depressed, when we are ill, when we are in poverty, when we are in flight. While others wander, Zen students return to their seats and meditate. So to us, meditation is our home.

On Sunday mornings we meditate; then, from this meditation, we go out to perform our life. The next Sunday, we return to meditate. When we are stricken with illness, we need meditation. When we have lost our position, we return to meditation. When we must risk our lives, we start with meditation. We always return to meditation.

In ancient days in my country, warriors came in the morning to meditate in the temples, then went out to the battlefields, fought bravely, and perhaps died. Warlords, when their castles were about to fall, seized by the enemy, returned to their meditation seats to meditate upon Emptiness.

When I was young, and it was examination day, before I went to school, I would close my books and go to my seat to meditate. If, in the examination, a very difficult problem appeared on the blackboard and I was in a quandary, I meditated to quench the palpitation of my heart, for I had found that my brain worked better after meditating.

Meditation is the final decision. Sometimes it is the first step toward death. You forget everything in meditation. To us, meditation is returning to the bosom of God. We are free from all external turmoil.

It is very difficult to practice meditation when you are in trouble; naturally, you have no courage to do it. You just run amok. It is better to practice before the mind is upset. Westerners are not in the habit of doing this. But to us, it is a completely natural thing to be quiet when we are in difficulty.

In Japan, about four hundred years ago the abbot of Erin-ji, Kaisen Osho, had a student and patron who was a famous warlord. I once went all over that temple with my teacher's brother and saw its huge gate, which is a building in itself. There is a large hall downstairs, and in the upper story is the *hatto* (the hall in which lectures on the sutras are given). We climbed many stone stairs, passed through this gate, then went along a path paved with stones to reach the main temple building.

Oda Nobunaga, one of the greatest warlords of Japan, attacked the followers of the warlord who was a patron of this temple. Some of the soldiers, under the leadership of a man named Sasaki, ran into the temple seeking refuge. The abbot gave them sanctuary. In ancient days, when an abbot accepted refugees into his temple, it was the unwritten law that he could not be forced to give them up.

The leader of the attacking force said to the abbot: "If you do not give up Sasaki, I will burn down the temple." The abbot refused.

The gate was set on fire. The five hundred monks and the abbot took refuge upstairs, and seated themselves in the posture of meditation. Without moving, they were annihilated in the *samadhi* of fire. It was at this moment that the poem was recited.

So to us, meditation is not only for quiet moments. To practice meditation, we cultivate our forces of courage and valor. When you are in some predicament, you join your hands, and with your prayers invoke God to guard you. You are very happy to have faith in a god who looks over you. We do not have faith in a god outside ourselves. We return to meditation. There is no running around in the fire, shouting or scratching at the wall, dying like a cat or a dog. We die accepting the fire. It is our faith.

I think this decision is very important in life. In 1932, though I did not say anything to any of the members of my temple, there was just one month's rent in the bank and not many people at my lectures. Today I see six people. At that time, six people were a crowd, and I would say, "Today was very successful." I was holding on by a hair. "One month more! Then I go somewhere else." I did not talk about it. If, when we are in a predicament, we speak about it and make a disturbance, we hinder the natural development.

I return to meditation. In the morning, I get up, sit on my couch, and meditate. Meditation is the conclusion of the Zen sect. Meditation is our religion. Speech is not the crystallized center of my sect. Meditation is the most sacred moment to us. You do not need to practice for hours. During the day when you start to do something, sit down, and the heart pumps in its natural rhythm. After you eat your food, meditate for five minutes quietly. Meditation is exactly like that.

When I went to Boston, a newspaperman tried very hard to make me say that Zen is the sect of the Japanese military. I just smiled and did not hop into his hand. I said, "I don't know if the Japanese Army knows about Zen or not!" But I say to my students: "Warriors have no time to work with complicated philosophy. Zen is their religion."

So Zen is important in this period.

This temple is very small, very poor. Today is Sunday. If between Monday and Saturday you come back for one moment to meditation, it will be like a drop of cool water to a bird. I am very proud of having kept this temple open for eight years.

THE ZEN SECT OF BUDDHISM

On February 22, 1936, I gave a lecture before the Japan Society of Boston. It seems to me they did not understand my address; they could not understand which was the tail, which was the head. Judging by the questions after the lecture, I must conclude that the intelligentsia of Boston could not understand what Buddhism is. I wonder if my audience in New York will be able to understand my lecture any better. Of course, I cannot repeat exactly what I told them, but I shall attempt to repeat it.

Before you understand what Zen is, you must understand what Buddhism is. I was born the child of a Shinto priest. Until I entered the Buddhist temple I did not know anything about Buddhism, though I had read the lines of the sutras. When I received the first koan from my teacher—"Before your father and mother, what were you?"—I used German philosophy as an instrument to solve it. I was preparing to take an examination to enter the Academy of Art in Tokyo, and as preparation I was studying aesthetics. Edouard von Hartmann was famous in Germany at that time. In his philosophy of the unconscious he emphasized the concrete microcosm. I took this viewpoint to solve the koan, and my answer was "Absolute." I answered incorrectly, so my teacher rang his bell at me—I was terribly disappointed.

Then I came back home and I took a materialistic view—before negative and positive and all relative existence that is based upon phenomena, there is just one solid existence, which is colorless. My second answer was "Transparent"—and my teacher rang the bell again. Disappointed, I walked around Tokyo, and, standing before a bookshop, I opened a paper and found a line of poetry translated into Japanese:

> O rose in the garden,
>
> I do not ask what you were in the past,
>
> Or what you will be in the future.
>
> Your existence is forever with God.

I did not like this "God," but certainly it opened my eye to an entirely different vista, and I walked into this avenue, found the gate of Zen, and opened it.

Three years later, I opened the sutras and studied Buddhism. When I knew the ins and outs of Buddhism, I could say Buddhism teaches you "what this is," instead of "what to do." To the question of "What to do?" Buddhists pay no attention; but we strive to know "what this is." [Lifts up glass—] "What is this?" [Beats table—] "What *is* this?" When I was a child I went to a Buddhist temple and listened to a monk giving a lecture. The monk lifted a teacup and said, "Gaze long enough at this and it will disappear." I went home and looked a long while at a teacup, waiting for it to disappear. It did not. My father asked what I was doing. I said, "I'm concentrating, waiting for the teacup to disappear, as the monk said." My father said: "That Buddhist monk does not know what he is talking about. He does not know the metaphysics of disappearance."

Turn the objective "What is this?" to subjective and ask this question of yourself. Then this question takes on a Buddhistic appearance. "What is this?" is the first question of Shakyamuni Buddha. He followed the Indian method of meditation and tried to understand this intuitively. He renounced the world and became an ascetic. This is the attitude of all Buddhist monks. Before concentrating on himself to find "What is this?" he renounced the world. He took such an aloof attitude because he did not want to find himself in a "pretty kettle of fish." In the first line of the *Samyutta Nikaya*—the oldest of Buddhist scriptures—there is this: "You ought to observe that *rupa* is ephemeral; that *vedana, samjna,* and *samskara* are also ephemeral. Therefore you must find something that is not ephemeral upon which to base your life." The question of mutability and how to get out of it and find eternity was a current question in that age, both in the Orient and in Greece.

As students we begin with the task of subjugating the first of the five *skandhas, rupa-skandha,* phenomenal appearance. When I was a child, I asked why the sky is blue. I was told because interstellar space is dark, so vibration of ether is not transmitted into light—light doesn't manifest except in the air. Space is pitch dark and we see this space through the atmosphere, so the sky is dark. This happens in air just twenty miles deep. Later this knowledge gave me a sense of the ephemerality of outer existence. (In Boston they could not understand what I was talking about at this point. I called Buddha the conqueror of the world of optical and mental delusion.)

If you study optics, it will prove to you what color is. You will see that what is usually seen as green, occasionally looks red, according to the condition of your eyes. Color does not exist out *there*—it belongs to the retina of your eye. You would say, "This color is red," "That sound is noisy," "Sugar is sweet," "A pin is painful,"—but the pin is not painful; pain belongs to the skin, not the pin. All sense perceptions are your perceptions and exist inside; what exists outside, God knows! Perhaps noumenon—noumenon and phenomenon.

Next is *vedana-skandha*—to feel outside. Outside and inside are like a box and lid. If you have no sense organs you cannot tell outside from inside. And then thoughts—*samjna-skandha*. Thought is very, very fine; it exists in your mind naturally. It is tenacious; you must exterminate it. How? You must use your brain to exterminate it. What is monism? What is dualism? What is pluralism? All this has value, but it has nothing to do with Reality, with Real Nature.

Then there's *samskara-skandha*. You find many translations given to *samskara*. One Western scholar translated it as "the accumulation of the creative element." Another translated it as "confection" or "confectioner." I did not understand this translation. I opened a dictionary and found it was "candy" or "cakemaker." I could not understand this at all until someone told me that some candy has seeds in it! This *samskara* does hold seeds—it is the seed-holder. When you are sleeping, *samskara dreams you*—you are not dreaming. We are *samskara*. We feel it as mood, emotion—all that we cannot control. If you observe this in the outer world it is very clear to you—the willow shows you its spirit by drooping its branches, and so forth—all the endless shades of the mood. It gives you a panorama in which you can live. But if you feel it in your mind it is only a wave of your consciousness.

What is consciousness? To meditate upon your pure consciousness—*vijnana-skandha*—you feel boundless space, then space gets into your consciousness and all the universe is your consciousness. It is like a mirror. Without anything to reflect upon the mirror, the mirror does not exist. Standing in front of the window of a New York department store, I see nothing in its reflection—then suddenly, I see a Japanese face—it is I.

The mirror in the sky that receives no reflection cannot prove its own existence, so consciousness disappears and enters into eternal Emptiness. But from this Emptiness all the universe will spring once more. The universe does not need to do anything to wake up again. And when this is carried out it is not yourself. *That* thinks, *that* comes—Tathagata, Great Nature, *that* which comes exactly as *that* wholeness of the universe. We also call IT Buddha Tathagata. And Buddha is the microcosm of that. He is the child. He was there as a child before *that* and when he came, he came exactly as *that*—the image of the father. You must understand how Christianity is analogous to Buddhism, but Buddhism is five hundred years older.

Then we come to this present conscious mind and material world—the flower is blooming, the bird is singing. I enjoyed this phenomenal world when I was young.

In the real experience of meditation, you will experience everything at once. When you are going up you are coming down. The youngest baby is the oldest man, and the oldest man is the youngest baby. For the baby has a long past but has just left it; and the old man is ready to be a baby again.

A story is told of two monks watching a current of water. One said, "It is circling to the center." The other said, "It is circling to the outside." Their debate was endless. Then a Zen master came and hit one of the monks in the eye and asked, "Which way is the water going?" And one of the monks answered, "All ways at once." So in meditation, you are converging to a point, and at the same time you are diverging to the kaleidoscopic universe. In the interval you will find yourself.

Another story is told of how Master Gutei held up one finger in answer to every question. "What is Buddha?" "What is Nirvana?" Gutei always showed his one finger. A young novice, imitating the master, held up a finger; the master promptly cut it off. The novice ran away, shrieking. The master called him back and raised his finger; the novice imitated him again. In that instant he was enlightened. He realized what this is.

There is Zen in the West also. When Dr. Johnson kicked a huge stone and said, "I refute *thus*," in response to Bishop Berkeley's statement on the subject of reality, that was Zen. I hope you understand. If you don't, no one understands Zen in Boston or New York.

BODHIDHARMA'S ZEN

To experience Bodhidharma's Zen, there is no need to destroy this existence—*you are facing everything*. Without making yourself a "single" existence, without making your consciousness into "nothing," you suddenly realize that *this* existence, "I and that," are your original nature, and that you cannot say a word about it, cannot divide *this* existence into two pieces—mind and matter. Of course, in that moment, all color, all sound—everything together, without changing the nature of mind and matter—disappears. This is what is known as sudden enlightenment, Bodhidharma's Zen.

THE ZEN TEACHERS OF CHINA

Many Japanese think that Zen is a grotesque religion, that the Zen teachers of China are grotesque. I do not feel this way. To me, Zen is very plain, and the Chinese Zen teachers were plain, honest men. Why do Japanese students feel that the Chinese teachers were like demons or savages living in the mountains? Perhaps to the Japanese, Chinese sentences have some grotesque nature, some sharp, strong force that is lacking in Japanese sentences, even though they are composed of Chinese characters. When I translate Chinese into English and then read the English version, my feeling about what is said is entirely different from my feeling when I read the Chinese characters. A Zen teacher must understand this when he is transmitting such a special school of Buddhism to Westerners. He must transmit Zen itself. As religion, Zen is pure, with no mystical or grotesque element in it.

When other teachers of Zen come after me to this country, they should note what I have just said about transmitting Zen to American people. They should not transmit that particular poetic feeling that comes from Chinese sentences. I am trying to transmit Zen itself, not Chinese literature, to American people.

MY FIRST KOAN

I entered the monastery in my twentieth year and was given a koan by my teacher Sokatsu Shaku, a disciple of Soyen Shaku, in February.

My first koan was: "Before father and mother, what were you?"

I struggled hard and gave an answer every morning, but each time, my teacher would ring me out.

At last, I had no more to say. Then my teacher said, "Before father and mother, there was no word. *Show me* that word!" I could not answer.

Near the monastery there was a lake, which took about one hour to walk around. One freezing night I went around and around until the break of dawn. I was going around for the third time, I think, when I paused, exhausted and absent-minded. Suddenly my heart whispered, "This SILENCE is your answer—enter." I stood still, fearing to think. Then I annihilated all words and stepped into SILENCE.

Later, as I sat before my teacher, he said, "Penetrate that SILENCE!" and he rang the bell. But I knew that he had recognized my SILENCE and had accepted my answer, as a man who digs and finds wet sand.

THE FOUNDATION OF
BUDDHIST PRACTICE

The Buddha taught the three basic principles of *shila, samadhi,* and *prajna,* that is, commandment, meditation, and the attainment of wisdom. By their practice, one attains freedom of mind and emancipation.

To act according to your true nature is *shila.* We usually translate *shila* as "commandment," but this is not a good translation. *Shila* is the regulation of mind action and physical action.

When a Japanese farmer channels water from a pond to a rice field, he regulates the flow of the water. When you eat, you regulate your intake of food: you might not eat all the food on your plate but only a portion of it. In the same way, you introduce into your mind and life what you need. In English, law means that someone has made a particular system, then commands others to obey it. But *shila,* in Buddhism, does not mean that teachers make laws and then command you to follow them. True nature commands us, so we do not need any teacher to command us. However, since we are in a state of delusion or handicapped by habitual desire, and are blind to the true regulation of the functions of body and mind, we begin training with the practice of commandment.

If you have just killed someone and fear the police are after you, how can you keep your mind quiet or think of attaining wisdom? If you are involved in unlawful relations with someone's wife or husband, how can you keep your mind quiet when you know that someone may have found out and be after you with a gun? As preparation for the practice of meditation, therefore, you must keep your body and mind free from fear. A simple precaution is to be sure that there is no police officer, no creditor, no injured party to answer to.

Of course it is possible to think or meditate even on the battlefield. In the rain of fire and blood, your mind can be quiet if you are trained. But this does not happen right away. At the sound of the guns, your instinctive reaction of the nerves is to tremble. Only through practice and experience can you attain great guts.

When I was a soldier in Manchuria, I tried to practice quiet mind from my first day at the front. I struck my stomach. "I am a Zen student," I told myself. "Why should I not be able to keep calm?" But the will to do it is not enough. Only practice brings freedom from fear.

Commandment is also connected with morality. To violate the rules of morality makes you feel that you have no standing in human society. To be a human being you must find solid ground under your feet.

In Buddhism, when you enter a monastery as a novice, they ask you to observe the minor commandments, which differ in every group. "You shall not lie, gossip, or accuse another of a fault" are common commandments.

The first practice in meditation, the second of the three foundations, is to drive the useless mind-stuff out of your mind. You are always getting carried away with it, rushing after every problem that comes up. When you go home from work in the evening, you sit down for a moment to quiet yourself, but the moment you pick up the evening newspaper, things come into your mind. How about this? What about that? And before you are aware of what is happening, your mind is jumping and jerking. The part of your mind that does this is important and useful, but it is also the source of your troubles. There isn't any trouble really. From the true view, politics, business, and gossip are all mind-stuff. While you are using your mind symbolically, that is, depending on names and comparisons, you cannot see Reality. See Reality first, then use your mind. The glass of water—what is it? This is this. That is all. There is just one Reality. Transcendental, actual—just names. Surprise the mind and see Reality directly.

When you talk, you need names, but in meditation you do not need a word. We start in naked silence. When you find real meditation without a word, you attain true wisdom. Your mind becomes pure, and you can see your true soul directly. When your mind is free from all conceptions that do not truly exist—Is it good? Is it bad? Is it giving or taking?—you will find true emancipation.

In Japan, there is a saying: "Punish the crime, not the man." This is some kind of talk, isn't it? How can you punish the crime and not the man?

There was a famous judge in my grandfather's time. A monk who had committed a crime was brought before him. "Confess everything you have done and I will punish the crime, but not you," the judge told him. The monk confessed. "Well," said the judge, "if you can abstract your crime from yourself, you can go free." The monk stood up and started home. "Wait," the judge said, "Where is your crime?" "It is written in your book. You can find it there." Of course he was a Zen monk. When you understand this, you really find salvation. But when you use words like Christianity, Hinduism, Buddhism, these are just words. When you know the one thing in the universe, you really find salvation.

In real salvation you attain the non-leaking mind. In English this has a strange sound. Leaking mind means that something is always exuding—desire, sensation, imagination. We must attain "no-leakage."

Desire is common to every human being. When you look at food and try to get it without permission, or bite off more than you can chew, we call this desire. To eat what you must to support your life is not desire. To bite off only what you can chew, the Buddhist calls regulation. I had a shameful experience when I was a very young novice. I went where there were many young ladies and tried to attract their attention. My teacher gave me a cuff. "It is not necessary to do that," he told me. That is leaking desire.

Desire distorts our observation. When artists look at a subject through some conception, they cannot make a pure portrait of the one who really exists. That is leaking sense perception.

Leaking imagination is the most difficult to exterminate. In meditation, you imagine: "Now I am in absolute oneness with Nirvana." *Thinking* you are "nothing" in meditation, or *thinking* you are in oneness—that you have really vanished—you drop your jaw, and someone looking at you can see you are in a terrible condition. Or, imagining yourself as Buddha, you expand your body through the universe. Most Buddhists experience this type of leaking imagination. It is not true meditation, but imagination. "I am in the air. I am nothing." This nothingness is not true understanding, but imagination. Drop this. It is dreadful; it is air—mind-stuff. It must be exterminated for you to become the true, pure entity that was made by God and not by the imagination of the human being. In a Zen monastery, if a student asks, "What is Buddha?" the master gives him a slap to open his eye and wake him up.

This teaching of the three foundations is very famous, for although it is Hinayana, it forms the basis of Mahayana Buddhism.

In the Mahayana period all the cardinal principles were expounded and explained. But we Zen students throw away names and terms that were made by human beings. Zen stands upon consciousness, not the sky or visible phenomena. When I show you a box, I do not call it either matter or spirit, existence or non-existence. It is the human being who gives names and makes distinctions. Zen students *actualize* consciousness in themselves, but cannot speak a word about it. However, when we wish to speak systematically about the stages of consciousness, we can borrow the terms used in the old accounts of Buddhism. For example, *alaya-vijnana* is the name given to the consciousness that lasts forever, or *adana* consciousness. *Adana* is the consciousness of the *arhat,* an enlightened being who is free of all desire.

As human beings, we have consciousness of the head; but we also realize that without our intention our hair grows and our food is digested. This is not human consciousness but nature's consciousness. As hungry spirits we have two consciousnesses: ever-starving mouth consciousness and nose consciousness. Then there is the body center for procreation. Psychologists call this sex, but we call it hell, the lowest consciousness. It is most useful and is essential for the continuance of human life; it is from the womb that other bodies are created. We have no sense of disdain toward this consciousness, but it is placed low, just as a kitchen utensil is kept near the sink, not on the shelf with the tea. We do not put it on top of everything.

We consist of all these consciousnesses, and they have three periods in which they come out: growing, staying, and decaying. Everything passes through these three stages just as clouds gather, flow, then fade.

People of the West think of their souls as something stationary, like a lump of sugar, but the Buddhists think of their souls as something that comes and goes, converges and diverges; its function is like that of a furnace.

Consciousness is flowing all the time, everywhere; it has no body and no mass. We see, believe, and use thoughts to perform actions, but they have no permanent body. This earth, too, is like the mind that flows.

The existence of the world is the mind of *alaya* consciousness; the mind located in our heads is the shadow of our real mind. According to the Mahayana explanation, it is with our *prajna* mind that we correct the distortion of our observation.

This explanation is a poor photograph we have made to explain our consciousness.

BUDDHIST STUDENTS

There are two kinds of Buddhist students. One kind prefers to attain wisdom; the other prefers to attain the completion of the deed. In the *Vimalakirti Sutra,* these two natures are explained. Both have their merits. Those who prefer to attain wisdom are philosophical; they are thinkers. The others, who prefer the completion of the deed, are usually called the religious type; they have the sense of Zen and are self-observers. They always feel a pang in their conscience; their daily life is a record of commandment. They will not kill a mosquito, nor do they hit a fly absent-mindedly, but occasionally they lack the understanding of why they must or must not do something. The law is written in their conscience, while the others, who are more philosophical, possess the law within their mind.

When you meet Buddhist teachers, you will find these two types. One has a keen understanding of Buddhism, but his daily life is rather careless; the other lives a good and careful life, but the point of each law is not quite clear to him. Thus, we always have two teachers in becoming a monk: one a teacher of the Dharma, the other a teacher of commandment. The teacher of the Dharma sets one's mind on fire and purifies it; the teacher of commandment washes one's heart with water and cleanses it. The one who has attained and teaches the Dharma, even though he knows that his words are wrong, must say something immediate to lead his pupil into Buddhism. So he will speak of the hypothesis of reincarnation and the wheel of karma, even though he knows that it is not ultimate truth. This is the agony of the teacher. The teacher of commandment also has his agony: he knows the perfect law and yet he occasionally violates it.

One of the great Mahayana teachers said: "One who violates the law of the commandment is a *bodhisattva.* One who has no commandment is not a Buddhist; he is a heretic." Commandment is both a keystone and a milestone. It is the milestone of daily life; we measure how close we are to it, or how far we are from it. The heretic does not have this milestone for the measurement of his conduct, and is not a Buddhist. Though you violate the law, you must find the milestone in yourself. To find it in your heart is your ultimate goal as a Buddhist.

You can say this or that to intellectual people, but you must have the true keystone of the entire structure of Buddhism in your mind. Then you will not mind people saying what is not true, for you will know the others' state and the error of their ways. You will know, even though you will smile and say, "Oh, yes!" that the statements of the others are in error. As a Buddhist, you will have a keystone in the mind and a milestone in the heart.

But it is not easy to find a complete Buddhist. To have both a keystone and a milestone, you must give yourself to Buddha's Dharma. Some will observe Buddha's Dharma from outside, or study it with their minds, or pretend that they have surrendered themselves. But only entire submission will attain both the milestone and the keystone. Christianity says that you must submit yourself to God's will—it is the same thing. Complete submission will attain the milestone and the keystone.

Then, in Zen terms, I will become "*Itself.*" If you wish to become a good husband, you must become your wife. If you wish to become a good mother, you must become your child. This is *yoga* (union). You are not yourself. You make complete contact with the object.

The term "submission" gives you a shade of humiliation—you must be flat on the ground. When you meditate on a koan, you surrender to it. An artist studies for many years and finally surrenders to Great Nature. To catch something of it, you must become it. You cannot catch it from outside, you must embody it. Then the things you wish to have are yours. To have a husband is the same thing. The true wife does not think of herself, but of her husband entirely. If she thinks of herself, he is not hers, for she cannot be him. But to realize complete submission, you must be very conscientious. You must understand the gesture of nature, you must see the shades of nature's handiwork, you must listen to nature's suggestion. As it is said in the common expression: Listen to the still, small voice within you. *It* leads you into complete submission.

The Buddha, when he was in the Bamboo Garden, told his disciples that there were four kinds of good horses. The best horse sees the shadow of the whip and runs; it sees the shadow of the driver holding up the whip in his hand, and before it is struck, it runs. The second-best horse runs when the whip touches its tail lightly. The third horse starts to run when the whip strikes its body. And the fourth horse does not run until the rider's spur penetrates to the quick; it stupidly remains standing until the rider's heel strikes its side.

A good disciple of the Buddha is like one of these horses. If a good Buddhist student hears that something has happened in town—someone has died in agony after a long sickness—the student thinks deeply and surrenders to it. Another thinks of the coming day when he will lose his mother or father. The third will have to come to the very day that his mother or father dies. And the fourth will have to experience the agony of death itself, or the crisis of a great earthquake, or the iron rain of battle.

These four are good students. They will think deeply and find the true meaning of the Dharma and surrender to it. They will listen to the suggestion of nature and complete their submission and find the body of commandment. Until that day, the teacher will not hand them the commandment. When a general completes his plan of strategy, he hands it to his officer. But if he doubts the officer's mind, he will not hand the plan to him. The officer must show his true and honest heart. Mere brainpower, or good technique, is not sufficient; the heart must be shown. Before the teacher of commandment hands down the entire commandment to the student, he must be sure that the student has the true milestone in his mind. Then he will leave all action to the student's judgment and will never doubt what the student does. In the same way, the Zen master's understanding is the same after the transmission of the Dharma. But to attain this complete submission to the suggestion of nature, great power is necessary. If you do not pass this point, you cannot have the body of commandment, or the mirror of Zen.

A heathen monk asked the Buddha, "I ask of you neither a word nor no word. Tell me directly, what is your Dharma?" The Buddha usually answered in silence or spoke a million words. In this case, the Buddha remained quiet a little while. This was his performance of quietude. He did not care what the heathen monk said. Then the monk said, "O Tathagata, you are the body of love and compassion. You have brushed away the cloud of illusion and made me enter into the Dharma." The heretic, filled with admiration, said this and left. Ananda watched him going and said, "My Tathagata, you did not say a word, but he said he had attained the Dharma. I wonder what he really attained." The Buddha said, "He is like a good horse when he sees the shadow of the whip." Just a slight suggestion and he completely opens his eyes and enters. He is a good student.

To attain so keen and clear and straight an entrance into the Dharma depends on your heart, which must practice submission and humbleness before the real truth. This real truth will manifest itself nowhere but in your own conscience, in your own brain; and when you get a suggestion from it, you must relinquish all notions, all conceptions.

Zen is a terribly intellectual religion, but the simplicity of it is the same as that of other religions that emphasize the pure heart. From either pure behavior or pure mind, you can come to the same point. If you try this once, then it will be easier for you day by day.

REPOSE OF MIND

You must understand one thing in Buddhism: there is no mystery in authentic Dharma. Some people misunderstand Buddhism. They think anyone who studies Buddhism will acquire supernatural power, not knowing the real meaning of "supernatural." Especially in America today, everyone wishes to have some form of power. They have enough power materially, therefore they wish to have some mental power. Their idea is to see through the wall, or to hear some voice the ordinary ear cannot hear. They are not trying to find repose of mind; their endless desire is to grasp something supernatural. I do not know what they would do with it if they had it. They are like children who wish to go to the circus— it is the childish element in their minds. Others think they will find in Buddhism the power to cure illness. They think Buddhism is a kind of hospital. But you must know that Buddhism is to bring repose to your mind. When you come to religion, you must relinquish your desire to possess power, material or spiritual. You must cultivate your immobile mind. Religion is simply for your soul. That is all. Religion is not for anything but the repose of your mind.

Religion is not knowledge by which you can make money or your living, which you can use for some purpose. No one expects a religious teacher to save money for some use. Religious teachers are always on the verge of poverty. Their life is given to them by their followers. If they have no followers, they must accept death. If they are afraid of death, they cannot be religious teachers. And, of course, religious laymen mustn't expect to make money from religion. It's more likely that they must *spend* their money for religion's sake.

When you come to religion, you are coming back to the home of your soul. When you come back home, you take a rest. You do not engage in any activity. This rest is the final goal of religion. To have this repose of mind, certainly you must gather knowledge of religion, but religion doesn't belong to knowledge—it belongs purely to the soul. It is like water: the reality of water is to be water—that is all. Of course, human beings drink water and prolong their lives; they dam the water and build factories, using the water's power to produce something; but water is not made for that. They are exploiting it, using it for their own purposes. Water is just water, and religion is just religion. Religion does not exist for any purpose. Religion is the place where you are born; religion is the place where you die; religion is the place where you are living. It is nothing else. There is no other element in it. To have a purpose in looking for religion, therefore, is wrong.

You must remember that to be religious, you must accept your present condition. If you are poor, you must accept that. If you wish to be rich, you must accept that also, and endeavor to be rich.

Of course, we study religion, but before we begin to study, we have faith in that religion. I studied Zen, but before I began to study Zen, I had faith in Zen. Faith is the mother of religion. Without faith, there is no religion. We study religion with an eager mind, with soul, with a warm heart, with deep thought, and with courage. Sometimes people study something in a very queer way. For instance, some study Sanskrit with the attitude of a baker baking a cake. It's just for the sake of business. When artists study art, they have love for it; they must have their hearts in it. So often those who study mathematics, philosophy, or logic study just as if it were a business. I cannot understand that attitude. When you study religion, you must not study in such a way! These days, students go to a theological college and become ministers, just like bakers baking cake. I cannot see how anyone can do that. How can their hearts be so cold?

My religion is plain and simple and quiet. Zen is the religion of quietude. Zen is not a complicated religion at all. It is plain. Well, why does it become complicated? Because you think Zen is some kind of theory or knowledge, some kind of philosophy, and you think you can do something with it. No, Zen is just: I am sitting here, and you are sitting there. This is Zen.

Repose of mind is the goal of all religious efforts. But repose of mind is not easy to attain. Of course, you must do something with your physical body—make pilgrimages, visit teachers, read and study the sutras—to find the conclusion. But the conclusion is the repose of your mind.

You must grasp the foundation that is your own mind—not universal mind, not the teacher's mind, not Buddha's mind—but your mind. It is yours. And then you must stay there. That is what makes religion.

MOONPRINT

When you are aboard ship, standing on the deck, you can look down and see a moonprint in the water. If you cross to the other side of the ship, you will see one there too. From the forward deck and from the rear, you can also see a round moon in the water. From wherever you look, it can be seen. You and every other passenger on the boat see a moonprint. Why are there so many?

Through many *kalpas* [eons of time], over and over again, I tried to grasp the moon's reflection in the bottomless depths of the empty ocean of mind, until finally I understood what the moonprint is. Of course, it is the "I." My consciousness, your consciousness, everyone's consciousness is a moonprint.

Without ridding your mind of religion, philosophy, conceptions, and delusions, you cannot understand what the "I" is. To reach Emptiness, you must practice meditation. Desire, anger, everything will be emptied by meditation. Then you will see your original nature. Empty Mind will transcend the dualistic phenomenal world, and at the same time, your egoism will be uprooted. "I, I, I, I, I," you will say; but there will be no I in the I.

THE BUDDHA SOUL SECT

We Japanese call our sect Zen. But Zen is not the original name of this particular sect. Before the Sixth Patriarch, Chinese Buddhists called it the Buddha Soul sect. This was Bodhidharma's name for it.

In the Sui dynasty [581–618] of China, a philosophical sect was dominant. A great monk, Chih-i [538–97], founded this sect on the "Heavenly Terrace" of T'ien-t'ai Mountain, which is in Chekiang province about one hundred eighty miles southeast of Hangchow. This mountain is shaped like an inverted eight-petaled lotus, with eight great ridges, eight valleys, and innumerable peaks. The sect was originally called the Lotus Sect because it was based on the *Lotus Sutra,* but it was renamed for the mountain. This sect takes a philosophical attitude but it is also based on meditation.

Another great sect was the Shingon or "True Word" sect, which came from China to Japan, and was derived from the Indian Yogachara School. In this sect the principles of Buddhism are expressed by symbols. It is a pictorial Buddhism, in which the symbols are systematically arranged diagrammatically into mandalas.

The Buddha Soul sect (Zen) made no diagrams or images, nor did it explain by philosophy. Zen Buddhists try to "feel" the Buddha Soul. Because we have IT, we feel IT.

To study the eye, we use pictures of it made from anatomical knowledge. Shingon Buddhism made pictures of the human soul, mind, and intellect by anatomical knowledge of it.

The Zen sect does not use knives to gain knowledge of the soul but introspects or looks into it. "Look into" is not the best expression to use here, for we do not really "look into" but "out of" the mental sphere, using the mind's inner eye, not our two eyes.

In the Zen school of Buddhism, we do not study anyone's mind but our own. Psychoanalysis is used to look at someone else's dreams or thoughts. We, day and night, "look into" our own mind. Psychoanalysts use mind-stuff as their material for study; we do not. We use mind activity itself.

When you make a gelatine dessert, first you pour it as a liquid into a concave mold, cup, or bowl. When it has jelled, you turn it upside down and remove the concave mold. The gelatine has been molded into a convex mass. Our mind-stuff is the concave mold. Our mind activity, feeling the outside impressions—heat, cold, joy, anger—takes on their convex form from this concave mold. When you are angry at making contact with something, your mind activity is poured into this concave form. It is the same with joy, when your mind is poured into the mold of laughter. Touching fire or water with your finger, feeling heat or cold, your mind is formed.

Psychologists study the concave mold. Our method is different. We sweep all the mind-stuff off, destroy all the molds. Then we find the original form of mind activity. It is not to be found in any meaning such as joy or sadness, high or low, abstract or concrete, relative or absolute—the pairs of opposites. These are just concave molds. We destroy everything. We take off all the concave molds and return to the original state of mind activity. It is as if the molded gelatine was put into a large pan and melted so its form or shape ceases to exist. This is our first study. The koans we give you are the dynamite to destroy your tenacious concave molds and bring your mind back to its original state. Then you sit and observe the activity of boundless mind.

You do not need to study the molds made by Buddhists of the past. You have to find your own mind activity. Do not jump from the frying pan into the fire. After you have broken your old mold, do not remold in some Buddhist pattern. Many teachings prevailing today are concave molds. You have enough molds as you are. Why take on another?

If I were to try to put your mind into another, it would be like taking you out of the form of a snake and putting you into the form of a skunk or something. You must not enter any ready-made concave mold.

If you really experience IT with your positive shining soul, you will really find freedom. No one will be able to control you with names or the memory of words—Socrates, Christ, Buddha. Those teachers were talking about consciousness. Consciousness is common to everyone. When you find your true consciousness, you will not need the names or words of any teachers. There is no particular concave soul. Once you are experienced, you will find the law for yourself. Do no put on anyone else's rigid form. Keep your mind free and look into the natural activity of universal mind. Words are a particular mold. So in the Zen school we hate words. When students use words to make molds, the teacher must destroy them.

You come into the Zen room with a pan on your mind. The Zen master knocks it off. Next day you come in with another pan, and he knocks that off. Pan after pan after pan. Even if you come in with a stove perched on your head, the teacher will smash it and drive you from the room. Finally, you find your mind's own activity. But even then you try to put it into a mold to show the teacher. Do you think he is blind? Unkind? When you come in with your soul bare, the teacher will see it. We do not want any formula as an answer. Each answer must be the student's invention, the student's creation.

Of course, we know the "best answers" historically. These have been handed down. When you have passed the koan yourself, the teacher will tell you these. There are philosophical answers also, which may be given to you after you have got the real answer, but these are not the "main store"—just the annex.

The Zen master uses kindness, shouts, or strikes. If he is disgusted, he just gives up on you. When I am intense, I am most kind.

Do not make a mistake. If I smile, it means I think the answer is insignificant. A true, substantial answer must be made by the student. Then I say, "All right." And I show you the best answers made by previous students. In my experience, when I show previous answers to students, they protest. Of course, this is due to their ignorance. The pupil should listen and accept, since it comes from the teacher.

When the teacher asks you a question, do not answer with philosophy. Give a true answer. Once a true answer is given, it is never forgotten. Sometimes a student will spend two, three, or perhaps even five months on a koan before passing it, then a year later will have forgotten his answer. In my experience, no real Zen student forgets answers. If you have forgotten, find the answer before the teacher asks you.

For beginners, I speak of mind activity. For three or four years this is enough. A Zen student would not call IT activity or mind or soul. If you call IT mind, it is not soul. If you call IT soul, it is not mind. Do not call IT by any name. If a fire is burning down your house, though you point at it and yell at it and become angry, it won't make any difference. The fire burns just the same.

We divide consciousness into three stages: *alaya* consciousness, the ocean of consciousness; *hridaya* consciousness, sleeping consciousness; and *citta* consciousness, present thinking consciousness.

Alaya is the consciousness of fire, water, air, ether, electricity. You can see the activity of this consciousness clearly. When you see this bowl, which I strike, to you it has no consciousness, but it has force, energy. If it is melted into fire, the fire will have the force to move something. From the outside, this bowl is matter, of course, but in *alaya* consciousness it has its own conscious law and its own conscious activity.

The words or names "matter and spirit," "material and spiritual," come from the Western world. Before the invasion of the East by the West, this dualism was unknown. There was no difference between matter and spirit. When I was a child, the ground was not mere earth, but spirit. The sky was not mere space, it was spiritual space. Since Western dualism came into the Orient, the world has become dualistic. We certainly regret it. We were taught that matter and spirit are one from the beginning.

When we die we return to *alaya* consciousness, the ocean of consciousness. The ocean is not water but waves. You do not travel through the water but through the waves of *alaya* consciousness. Running from the fire that bars your way, you feel it as consciousness all around you. When you burn, your mind enters *alaya* consciousness.

Hridaya consciousness is more complicated, more sophisticated. All things that sleep are in this stage. The child at its mother's bosom does not know front from back, up from down, space, time, motion, dark, or light. Its consciousness does not exist, but you cannot deny its existence. If I ask you, "What were you then?" Would you answer, "I cannot remember"? The sleeping stage is a wonderful state. There is no individuality in it. All sentient beings are in this one stage, are one in it. It has its own activity, and we live according to its law.

Citta consciousness is this present thinking consciousness, which we control with our awareness. We look; we see the enemy. He runs, we run from him. Even cockroaches are in the *citta* stage. I observe cockroaches quite intellectually. If one feels danger, he runs. If alone, he comes out like a pickpocket. The cockroach mind is different from that of an onion or a pine tree. We do not have to speak about our *citta* consciousness because we know it so well. We feel it directly.

We use these three consciousnesses—*alaya, hridaya,* and *citta*—as a base and find *prajna* consciousness. It is not so difficult, if you get into the center of *alaya* consciousness. Do not stick around here or look for a different mold. Do not let your mind get into any dead words; they are just molds. Gather yourself into the center that stands like an incense stick, and penetrate through the three stages. At the top is the *prajna* stage, but the *prajna* state is different from the other three. From sleeping to waking to consciousness to shining—then you will really find freedom and no name can mean anything to you. Aristotle, Christ—all the great teachers talk about consciousness, but when you find your own consciousness, you will be yourself.

HOW TO PUT ZEN INTO SPEECH

For three or four years I have been thinking about how to put Zen into words, how to explain to Westerners precisely what Zen is. I am not quite ready to speak about Zen in entirely new terms that are unlike those traditionally found in orthodox Buddhism, but perhaps I can make an outline that will guide people to the gate of Zen. For before they begin the discipline of Zen, they need to become acquainted with this entirely new thing in the West called Zen.

First, I have tried to locate the essence of Buddhism. There are two different ways to approach truth in the world: one is through philosophy, including science in a broad sense; the other is by prayer, as practiced by the saints of old, who knelt in the desert sand or in the woods, concentrating in solitude. I do not know how Jesus found this method in the desert, but afterward in many places he would pray to his Father in heaven. He reached to God through that device. This happens many times to those of religious experience. Also to artists or musicians—suddenly inspiration comes to someone who is playing the piano, for instance, and he will leap out of this everyday existence, reaching a higher stage than that of daily life.

Buddhism, from the Buddha's time, did not take either of these two attitudes, the philosophical or the supplicating, to reach the higher stage, or God. These schools were already in existence. The Tantric schools used incantations—though they did not evoke with the lips but with the mind. The Brahmans' efforts were to go there from here, concentrating on the spatial difference between their own position and the place they must reach. The Buddha's attitude was not philosophical and was not a reaching out to someplace. He tried to face actuality *here*. He tried to find something that was true within himself.

It is not necessary to think in words. You do not need to reason to find your nose. Nor do you need to say, "O, Father in heaven, please help me find my nose." You just find your nose on your face. That is how the Buddha tried to find the truth in himself. I think a Zen student understands this immediately. When you find your true aspect, it is not by philosophy or prayer. Your true aspect is not before you or behind you or beside you. It is in you. It is in the place where you are standing, and you cannot separate it from yourself. This is a very old way of finding yourself, but it is still new.

Philosophy tries to find the truth with words. There is no philosophy without words, you know. And science tries to find it outside. Looking at the world through a microscope, the scientist sees the whole universe in his fingernail, all ridged and valleyed. But he sees it as outside himself.

Both philosophy and science are like an old man with a cane. They have no strength in themselves. Buddhism doesn't lean on a cane but stands on its own feet and walks without a cane. It can go through the philosophy place, the science place, or any place.

From the first page of the sutras, Buddhism is full of logical contradictions. You can say, "There is nothing in the universe, and there is everything in the universe" at the same time, for logic doesn't mean anything in Buddhism. From the Buddhist point of view, you can say, "I do not exist, and I exist," and the proof is that you are standing there.

Now, we come to Zen. What is Zen? How can we speak about it using everyday words? Let us take the metaphor of the Trinity, the triune body, and apply it to material existence. Water, frozen, is ice, a solid; evaporated, it is steam. The trinity of water is: solid, liquid, vapor. If you squeeze vapor, you can reduce it to liquid. Crystallize liquid, and you cannot find the liquid any more; it is solid. Once the diamond was a gas that became liquid. Then solid. Strange, isn't it? This is the Father, the Son, and the Holy Spirit in the material realm.

If we use this metaphor to think about our thoughts, there are solid thoughts, liquid thoughts, and atmospheric thoughts. Sometimes we say people living in New York City are really living in matter, between bricks and stone, cement and concrete. But if you go to the cement maker, you can speak with him about cement, but not about New York. If you go to the brick maker, you can talk with him about bricks, but not about New York. You can see stone in a mountain quarry, but New York is not there, for New York is not brick, stone, cement, or concrete. New York is thought expressed by matter. All around us are buildings, bridges, and subways—all solidified thoughts, thoughts expressed by solid matter, solid thoughts. My *hossu* whisk is wood and horsehair, but when I hold it, it is my thought cast in solid matter.

Some people prefer nature to the city, but I myself prefer human thoughts expressed in matter to the unformed thoughts of nature. I see nature in them. Of course, my attitude is different from yours. I objectify this brush that originally was in an unformed stage, just as a patriarch, seeing people as so many trees on a mountain, observed their movement as the movement of nature.

You can objectify your thoughts into a liquid form also. The liquid expression of thought has no solidity of form. Yet, flowing from the lips to the ears, it creates waves and whirlpools. What was it that happened in Russia? It wasn't just words, was it? Bolshevism was like a tornado or a tidal wave. Fascism, too, was like a wave of dense liquid, stronger than words.

Everything you think with words might be called liquid thought. Its consistency is like strawberry ice cream. Pictures are not quite solid, not quite liquid. They stand between the two. Sculpture is solid.

Atmospheric thought cannot be put into words, into form. It is lost when it is put into words. The poet understands this very well.

Perhaps music is liquid thought, but it is atmospheric, too. You cannot grasp any meaning in it. Its meaning is tangible but not definitely expressed. And religion—when you say God, Buddha, Allah, or when you put it in semiliquid matter, it is just G-O-D. It does not convey the meaning of your religious experience. Jesus strove three years to explain it in words, but he could not do it. Then his disciples tried for two thousand years to put it into words, but it cannot be carried by words. You can feel the meaning, but it cannot be conveyed in words. Atmospheric thought—that is the wonderful part of religion.

A Japanese friend who lives in the suburbs came to visit me. He said, "Your place is under the elevated train and on a noisy street, but it is very quiet. In the suburbs, where I live, there is no noise, yet it is very noisy. How do you get it so quiet?" I told him, "It is my thoughts that are quiet." When I was sitting here and he was sitting there, there was something that kept his thoughts relaxed, and it *was* quiet—as quiet as a temple in Japan.

And now we come to the Zen "atmosphere." We cannot express this in words, but you feel a million words that are unspoken. All religion is here. It is the same as poetry. It is the whole triune body.

Not only Buddhism, but almost all religions are atmospheric thought. Philosophical thought is liquid; art is semisolid and semiliquid thought. When you have a thought that is atmospheric, you have to press it to make it into a liquid and then compress it and make it solid—concrete. The tendency of the human mind is to begin with the liquid form. When you taste this, you become intoxicated and go both ways, solid and atmospheric.

Now I'm going to tell you how a Zen student develops the triune body of thought.

When you have been given the first koan, "Before father and mother, what were you?" you conceive an atmospheric thought first by meditation. You think about it. But it cannot be put into words. It is beyond space and time. If you put it into solid form immediately, one million years in one second—well, all right. This is the past, present, and future, beyond time and space. You have gone directly from the atmospheric to solid physical matter.

But if you bring a liquid thought as an answer, the Master will slap you to bring you to a solid. For, by hitting you, he hits the whole universe. Of course, the blow is not personal, not done to satisfy his anger. After you have proved your answer, the Master may say, "Express it in words." But if you say, "It is beyond time and space," the Master will answer "R-r-ring!" with his bell. Your answer must show insight.

A man asked me,

"Why do you always stay in the Green Mountains?"

I smiled, but I did not answer.

A peach blossom follows the stream a thousand miles.

This is a famous poem. To taste such a poem, you must have the highest kind of thought, the endless feeling of Zen.

So, first, you have atmospheric thought; second, put it into a solid; third, bring it back to a liquid.

In ordinary life, usually your thoughts are liquid first, then they go through the atmospheric stage, then solidify, for this is the Western way of thinking. Yet it is first atmospheric, then solid, then liquid. If you really think about this, you will be able to understand how to make a Zen answer. Once you understand Zen, it is easy.

BODHIDHARMA'S
TWO ENTRANCES

The "gate of reason" and the "gate of practice"—Bodhidharma's two entrances—are the foundation of Zen. I am not sure if the word "reason" is a good one to use here or not—but I shall use it this once. Reasoning is not physical practice, it is mental activity. By this mental activity, we arrive at a conclusion; from this conclusion, we perform our action in daily life.

Every religion has these two gates. In Christianity, God is the gate of reason, love is the gate of practice. With the understanding reached by the gate of reason, we perform our daily life. If we perform without it, we perform blindly and make terrible errors. I am sure I do not need to repeat the details of the Oedipus story—how Oedipus killed his father and married his mother, without knowing—I shall merely point out that it is an illustration of man's blind life.

The gate of reason in Bodhidharma's theory has no end. It goes only so far and then enters chaos—there is nothing at the end of it. This is a wonderful part of Buddhism. The summit of the triangle has no ultimate, it is endless. There was a story—an English poet told this—of a man who traveled over mountains to find the end of the world. On his way he passed many temples. After a while, he came to a place where he was told: "This is the end of the world." But he did not believe it and went on. Finally, he reached the real edge of the world—a great cliff. There he saw the chaos of the infinite and couldn't take another step. This is an allegory about the end of reason. When we are thinking about the highest truth, we think and think and think until we come to the ultimate; then we cannot think anymore. Our thinking mind can go no further; it is at the edge of a great cliff. Our thinking mind cannot step forward. This is the end. If you are thinking about something, you must come to this end of thinking. When you have something more to think about, it is not the true end. It is not through thinking about it that you see Truth. You cannot feel it or think about it. When you come to the true end, you stop thinking and you see Truth. It is not thinking of Truth, it is not looking at Truth as a picture. You *see*.

It's like using a drill. As long as you can drill, it is not the end.

When there is no resistance left, when you can drill no more, it goes "Ztt!" and the end is reached. We say thought has penetrated through reason. When you have reached the true conclusion, there is no word. When you have destroyed the last word and arrived at chaos, it is the infinite. If you come to God or Buddha or anything, it is not the end. But when you have destroyed the last word, when you cannot think of anything more, then you will see that endless gap.

Perhaps you will turn back because you are afraid. But the Zen student is not afraid; the Zen student will leap into the infinite. You must jump into it. Just jump! Not with your body—your body still sits where it is, so you need not be afraid. Jump into that conclusion.

While you have a word, you are not a good student. While there is some picture in your brain, you have not reached the end. If you have a lotus flower in your hand and are mounted upon an elephant, you are dreaming. If you think that God sits upon a cloud with Peter and Mary on each side, and Christ is in front of you on a throne, you have not come to the real Truth yet—you do not see the real God. You are thinking about it, but you don't *see* it. You are looking at something, so you haven't come to the end yet. As long as you are thinking something is there, and you are thinking about it, it is not the real end. But when there is nothing to think about, and your faculty of thinking has come to an end, and you all of a sudden throw yourself into chaos—into the infinite—your mind and body and soul all disappear. That is the real end.

In ancient times, students experienced this by meditation; today we experience this by *sanzen*. But if you practice with both methods, it will be as if you are a tiger with wings. If a tiger had wings, what would such a tiger be? The ox is very slow, the horse is very fast. The ox has horns, the horse does not. But if the horse had horns, the horse would be better than the ox.

Shakyamuni's enlightenment under the Bodhi tree is an example of entering the end. He proved Nirvana. There is nobody whose name is God, whose name is man, neither devil nor demon, who lives in Nirvana. Nirvana is infinite, boundless.

That is one gate, one side. From there you come back to this life, to the entry of the practice of daily life. Right performance of daily life is the first duty. It is very interesting to see this in Oriental life. The Oriental attitude greatly differs from the Western.

There are four attitudes of performing daily life that are very important for the Buddhist. Compensation is the first. The second is to act in accordance with the course of nature. In the Buddhist sense, "course of nature" may perhaps read "course of karma." The third is to expect nothing. The fourth is to act in accordance with the first principle (*dharma*).

Compensation means paying back old debts from past deeds. Day by day we pay back debts of old karma. For instance, a woman is talked about badly. Gossip and rumor spread. Wherever she goes, everyone laughs and no one takes her seriously; in business, everyone despises her and will have nothing to do with her. What would you do if you were this woman? Would you stand on the corner of the street and say "I didn't do it?" Or would you advertise your innocence in the newspaper and explain it to the whole world? In such a case, the Buddhist takes the attitude that it is an opportunity to pay back old debts for something done in the past, or for some element in the mind or character. Say it is a religious teacher who has come to this city, opened a temple, and no one comes. He must think: "I am paying back some unknown sin I committed in the past." Well, if no one comes, he accepts it without a word, not trying to explain. Day and night, month after month, he accepts it in silence until it comes to an end. Until that time, he just sits down and waits until the debt is paid. If you have ego in your mind, you cannot do this. But if by the gate of reason you have annihilated the ego, you can say: "I did commit a crime in the past, and now they are talking about *it*, not about *me*. It is the karma of human life, not of a human being. We are all like waves in the ocean of karma, so we are in the center of the movement of karma. We must move with it and not complain." But if he thinks no one will believe in him and he cannot teach because he committed some sin in the past, this will give a nauseating feeling to the listeners. They will say, "Have you heard him? He isn't bad as a speaker, but there is something about his attitude I can't stand. It makes my blood boil."

When anyone talks about you badly, just meekly accept it. Say nothing, don't explain, not even to your friend. Silently accept it. Don't repeat a word. And when something good occurs, you don't need to advertise or boast of it either. It is like the sun and moon: they rise and set when the time comes. Thus, every moment of the day is compensation for past karma.

The second attitude of performing daily life is to act in accordance with the course of nature. The wind is blowing. You wish to light a cigarette. What do you do? Strike a match in the wind? No, of course not. You seek or make a sheltered bit of air. You strike the match and carefully shield the light. It is so plain. Do everything in accordance with the course of nature.

The third attitude is to do everything without expecting a result. When you accomplish something, you might expect appreciation. Perhaps you have made money, so you say to your children, "See, my children, what I have made." And your children will say, "Give me that money." Or you expect something for everything you do. "Oh, Reverend, I gave eight dollars. That is three dollars more than usual." Do not expect compensation for each good deed. You may not reap any reward for your deeds, but someone will. And for someone else's good deed, you will receive the harvest. Do the best you can without expecting any return. If something returns to you, it is like receiving a gift; if it doesn't, it is like lending money to someone. The reincarnation system is a wonderful way to explain the action of this principle.

The last attitude is to do everything in accordance with the first principle. Don't put your trust in God, then pray: "Oh, God, give me a nickel." Do the best you can. When we worship, we kneel down within and join hands with fear, with joy, and with awe to the infinite. And then we come back and live in the four attitudes, without ego.

I am accepting the law of compensation in accordance with nature. The life of compensation is the life of accordance with the course of nature, the life of not expecting any harvest. I am like an artist who makes beautiful pictures on sand. I am making something, and I am happy doing it. And if you rear a child, don't expect anything from it. You see a dog with her puppies. Does the mother dog expect anything from her puppies? No, she doesn't expect a thing.

To conclude: Do not do anything except in accordance with the first principle. The first three attitudes are included in the last, so in the end, there is only one attitude. This brings happiness and peace.

DEPENDING UPON NOTHING

If you wish to understand Oriental religion, you must know something of the development of the Oriental mind. Primitive societies in the Orient developed rituals to purify body and soul. After the tribes had gone hunting and returned from the fields—their naked skin stained with the blood of animals—they would quarrel over dividing the game. Later, they washed away the blood and made peace among themselves. They wanted to calm their disturbed minds before they appeared before the shrine of their deity. After washing the body and calming the mind, they could associate with each other, and sit before their deity. This ablution and meditation was a method of purifying their physical and mental body. I think all religions of the world have this type of practice. Besides this purification, they later offered fire and incense to God to purify the air.

If you go to China or Japan, you will see people in the summer evenings making huge fires to drive away insects or bad odors. If you stand near the fire, you can see the insects showering into the flames. Then, after purifying body, mind, and air, they strike a gong, light incense, and listen to the talk of the priest. It is like a New Yorker coming home from his job; he takes a bath and changes his clothes. Then he sits before a radio and smokes a cigarette to calm his mind before going to dinner. The method differs, but at bottom the purpose is the same. The Oriental washes and meditates and makes a fire. The Buddhists thought that if they purified the mind, they would attain enlightenment—that if they became wise, wisdom would penetrate everything. So they practiced meditation to obtain more wisdom.

In the Buddha's time, this exercise—meditation—was called *dhyana*. Today, we call it Zen. The word meditation is not exactly equivalent to *dhyana,* but for the time being, we use it. Among the monks in the Buddha's Sangha, there were some who practiced nothing but *dhyana*. Later, they became *dhyana* or Zen masters. They attained the wisdom to see through everything and to understand the origin of life and death.

My sect is the Zen sect. We practice meditation to purify the mind and to conquer thoughts. To conquer thoughts, we use wisdom, and when we conquer all thoughts, we have purified our minds. Then we are ready to attain enlightenment and tranquillity.

What shall we depend upon? What shall we meditate upon? This is always a problem in the beginning. When one of his disciples asked the Buddha about this, he answered: "You ought to practice real Zen. Do not practice strenuous Zen."

The answer is very short, but it is a very good answer. Of course, the disciple asked the Buddha the meaning of "strenuous Zen," for it was not a common expression.

The Buddha answered: "If you keep a horse in the stable, he is trained for the stable. If you take him into the house, he will be looking for his hay—he will be kicking the floor and making a clatter all night. This will awaken the people who are sleeping in the house. The monks who practice 'strenuous Zen' are exactly like that horse. When I am living with them, it is like living with a wild horse. I am so uncomfortable, I cannot stand watching it. My disciples, if you keep the horse in the stable, the horse will not be thinking all night of hay, or of the grass and beans outside the stable. The horse will stand still and sleep quietly—thinking of the master, of the carriage, and of the road." I am not so sure this is what the horse was really thinking, but the Buddha felt it was—and the Buddha should know the horse's mind. The monks then understood that they must keep quiet and not practice meditation so restlessly.

When you go to Japan and see monks practicing meditation, you cannot help laughing at them, they practice so strenuously. Their faces look like the faces of *arhats*.

The Buddha said: "The monks who practice Zen according to the instructions of the Buddha meditate upon earth, upon water, upon fire, upon air, upon *akasha* (space), upon consciousness, upon nothing, upon no-place, upon thoughts, upon no-thoughts. They do not depend upon this world. They do not depend upon the other world (death). They do not depend upon life or death, nor upon the sun (present consciousness), nor upon the moon (subconsciousness). They do not depend upon sight or sound or awareness or cognition. They are not trying to attain anything. They are not trying to search for anything. They are not following their awareness. They are not following conceptions. Thus they practice meditation."

Earth means daily desire—the desire to have, to sell, to buy. Not to depend upon desire is the first practice to purify the mind. All this struggle of life is useless; it comes from egotistic desire. An apple tree does not struggle because it has no egotistic desire. The human being is worse than an ape. Throw a peanut into a monkey cage, and five or six monkeys will rush to get it. When one gets it, the others give up. But not human beings. Human beings continue to struggle. They are worse than monkeys. They do not want anyone to have what they themselves cannot get.

Water is flowing thoughts. When we are talking, that is water. We are living in thoughts. From our standpoint, all of New York— its buildings, the subway, and the elevated trains—is not merely material, it is solidified thought. We use material to express our thoughts. So, when we come to New York, we understand the thoughts of New York. When we go to Seattle, we understand the thoughts of Seattle. When we go to Japan, we understand the thoughts of Japan. When we see how people dress—well, once it was their expression. These days, it is the expression or thoughts of the factory. Today we do not manage to make our own clothes and express our own ideas with them. Perhaps it is economical, but I do not think it is as tasteful as it once was.

Fire is emotion, mood, temperament. Everyone has a different degree of fire.

And air is consciousness. We cannot see it; it exists forever.

When the Buddha said: "They do not depend upon this world. They do not depend upon the other world," he was referring to life and death. Life and death are just like the front and back of a sheet of paper. You cannot separate one from the other. There are two surfaces, but they are really one. Close your eyes, it is death; open your eyes, it is life. You cannot depend upon either.

When you are not searching for anything, desiring anything, attaining anything, you meditate depending on nothing. Of course, if you depend on nothing, you are still depending upon something. This expression means, do not depend upon *anything*—that is real Zen. But to get to this conclusion, you must practice these measures one by one.

First, you meditate on desire. When I was a novice, we monks practiced begging from door to door. All of us were from good families, but we had to practice as mendicants. This was how we meditated upon desire. We realized what desire was as we stood upon the doorstep and begged for food. At each door it was different. We were taught to stand at the door like an elephant. We were not to have any desire to get or not to get. We were just to chant, to remain the same, whether someone worshiped or refused. At the next door it might be: "Go away," or "I am sorry," or it might be a beautiful young woman. We wore big umbrella hats so no one could see our faces; we were to look at everyone as though we were cows—never to thank anyone as a human being does, never to smile. That is the way we practiced meditation upon desire.

Then would come meditation upon thoughts. And so on. Finally we would come to the conclusion: Do not meditate upon anything. The Buddha said that if you meditate in such a way, you are truly meditating. Then all the *devas,* all the angels, will worship you, joining their hands and saying "*Namu!*" ("Hail!")

An old monk, with many wrinkles on his face, who was standing behind the Buddha and fanning him with a fan made of white feathers, said: "I am wondering about those *devas* who worship someone who practices meditation depending upon nothing." The Buddha said: "When you conquer all thoughts and come to the conclusion depending upon nothing, you are ready to be emancipated, truly free." If you depend upon nothing, you will understand God, understand the secret of human life.

The Sixth Patriarch said: "Depending upon nothing, find your own original nature." To do this, you have to conquer all thoughts, fight with all the difficulties of thought. If you do this, you are above thoughts. You are your own master, a king. No wonder the *devas* will worship you!

SOME TERMS THAT EXPLAIN BUDDHISM

There are some terms that are very important to Zen students—mantra, *dhyana,* and *prajna* are three.

Mantra is translated as "all-holding" or "holding everything," expressing all meaning in one word. Usually a mantra doesn't have any meaning in itself. For instance, this mantra [here Sokei-an chants] doesn't have any particular meaning. Or take "OM." In that one word are held all thoughts between heaven and earth; so we call it a mystic word.

There are words in Zen that correspond to mantras. A Zen master asked the question of a disciple: "What is the white ox of the bare earth?" "White ox of the bare earth" is a Zen expression. It is ordinarily used, as Zen uses elephant, dragon, or tiger, to express some Zen viewpoint. "Venomous dragon" is often used as a name for a Zen master. "White ox of the bare earth" is one of the expressions by which we denote the state of *Samantabhadra,* the state of wholeness, the state of equality (*Samanta* means "sameness," *bhadra* means "wisdom"). To the question, "What is the white ox of the bare earth?" the monk answered, "*Ko, Ko!*"—the Chinese equivalent of "Moo, Moo!" Very simple! But in this case "*Ko, Ko*" corresponds to a mantra. In this word the monk expressed all thoughts that exist between heaven and earth.

Some Zen students in Japan think all koans are mantras, for instance, "MU." The students say, "All my koans are mantras." But this is erroneous. It is an amateur's, a dilettante's, view. Every expression of this type is not a mantra, but some expressions in Zen are analogous to mantras. Sometimes in *sanzen* we use these types of expressions. But do not use such expressions when you do not know what you are talking about.

Dhyana is Zen itself, so I shall not speak about it. In the *Sutra of Perfect Awakening* it is explained very carefully. *Prajna* is translated into English as "wisdom," but really the English word "wisdom" does not come to the point implied in *prajna*. It is a very important word, so I shall explain it.

This wisdom is omnipresent wisdom. To speak of omnipresent wisdom sounds very strange perhaps, but it is the wisdom of the universe. It is like saying heat is omnipresent. In interstellar space, heat is equalized, so the result is no heat, yet heat is everywhere. *Prajna* is like ether; it exists from the beginningless beginning to the endless end; it existed before anything was created.

Now, when I say *prajna* is wisdom, the statement is not very clear. Why call it wisdom? Because it is with the power of wisdom that we recognize existence. Therefore, this wisdom can be called "cognizance." When everything is in a state of equality, when everything is exactly the same, this wisdom doesn't function with cognizing power, for there is nothing to cognize. But if something is slightly changed, then this wisdom instantly cognizes that. When heat is equalized in interstellar space, there is no heat, but if energy is concentrated in one spot, it is cognized immediately. If my mind, your mind, everyone's mind were the same, I wouldn't recognize you and you wouldn't recognize me; we recognize each other because we are different. But the basis of mind is the same. When you die, this wisdom still exists, it does not decrease. But your physical body decomposes, so this wisdom loses the medium through which it functions. You always have the power to see, but if you lose your eyes, you lose the medium through which this seeing-power functions.

Now, why is *prajna* so important for Zen students? Because without *prajna* we cannot attain *satori*. The word *satori* is not to be found in English. To say "without *prajna* we cannot attain *satori*" means that without this wisdom we cannot cognize salvation. If you really understand these two powers, *samadhi* and *prajna,* your Zen is over.

When you meditate, it means that you discipline and train yourself in the practice of *samadhi,* you cultivate your power of quietude. Every day, every moment, you have to sit down and practice meditation. Just as you practice to shape your body, so you exercise in quietude to change the shape of your mind. But just meditating doesn't make Zen. You could meditate for a hundred years, but it doesn't make Zen. Only by the power of *samadhi* will your intrinsic wisdom awaken within you.

We have said that *samadhi* produces *prajna,* but *samadhi* does not truly produce *prajna. Samadhi* brings forth *prajna. Prajna* is there; it is everywhere. While we are sleeping, while we are eating, while we are drinking—in every state *prajna* is there, but it is covered by the turmoil of the mind. So, when you practice *samadhi* in quietude, the original quietude, the original *prajna,* which is innate, appears, just as your intoxication goes away and your sober mind appears. "Oh!" you say, "I remember hitting somebody! I hit Joe without any reason!" And you ask your sister, "Did I hit Joe?" "Oh yes," she says, "you gave Joe a big black eye!" And soberness appears.

So, in meditation, practice *samadhi* always; then *prajna* will appear. *Prajna* is not to be attained; *prajna* appears in your mind. You will say: "Oh, I see! I was looking for it a long, long time. I was seeking it for many years. How foolish I was! It is here. This is the state of *prajna,* right here." That is wisdom.

In *samadhi,* when *prajna* appears, you have attained *dhyana,* and in *dhyana* you utter a word: "Ha!" It makes a mantra. That is all. This is called Zen. A very simple thing, very simple. In koan work you practice *prajna, samadhi,* and *dhyana* in every circumstance.

Kumara-sudhana went to see Megha-bhikshu, an enlightened monk, on a mountain, but could not find him—just as you might try to find Rip Van Winkle in the Catskills. He looked seven days and seven nights but could not find him. So, in desperation, Kumara-sudhana went up another mountain—just as you, failing to find Rip Van Winkle in the Catskills, would go to some other mountain—"Ah, Megha!"

This is a koan: "How did Kumara-sudhana meet Megha-bhikshu on another mountain?"

You try to find him in the Catskills, in the Green Mountains, in the White Mountains, but you cannot find him. Then in deep meditation the mountains disappear; all the mountains become the same mountain. And then *prajna* appears: "Oh, I have met him!"

Do you understand my story? If you do not, you need some deep meditation. Then you will say "Hello!" and it will be a mantra. That "Hello" will mean everything between heaven and earth.

I think you understand why *prajna* is so important in meditation. Without meditation you cannot find *prajna.* When you once find it, however, you can never discard it—just as your heel goes with you wherever you go. You will enjoy this *prajna* when you find it.

ZEN AND THE RELIGIOUS FEELING

I was the child of a Shinto priest, and as a child I had faith in the Shinto God. The Shinto God has no physical body; he exists everywhere—he is not localized in any particular place. He is omnipresent, omnipotent, and omniscient. To my childish mind, the Shinto God was wonderful and infinite; he protected us in every way. A Shintoist does not believe in a god who punishes. He believes that if he commits an error, God will feel very sorry about it.

It is also believed in the Shinto religion that a personal soul, which is sacred and has force, will become a god after death. The soul of a warrior or of an emperor, it is believed, will be such a god after death. Shintoism has eight million gods and goddesses. When I first became acquainted with Christianity, I felt that it was rather logical that there was a jealous god in the world. With all those millions of Shinto gods about, I could understand there being one god who was jealous. Unlike the Christian, however, the Shintoist never thinks of angels.

When I entered the Zen faith, I realized there were no gods or goddesses, and no angels outside of us. Zen teaches that God is yourself. Christian Science and the Quakers teach that God is within us, but Zen teaches that God is yourself. Your self is God. It is not necessary to discuss within or without.

I felt at first that the universe had become very small, squeezed within my size, and I did not enjoy that feeling. A Christian who enters Zen must also feel that God is very small when squeezed within himself. I am certain you cannot press your hands together and worship yourself immediately, because you feel very small and discouraged. You feel that there is nothing that you can do to invoke God in your prayers; you feel that you are lost and have become faithless and godless.

I fought against this feeling of helplessness for a long, long time. I thought there must be some way out of this helplessness if I had this small, miniature god, which is myself, in myself. It is not easy to take seriously the idea that God is yourself, that you yourself are law, that your mind is law, that your body is law. Before such thoughts as these, we can lose the religious feeling. Oh, it is logical enough. We accept the idea as the conclusion of logic and reason. Perhaps we think we will have to discard the religious feeling of inspiration and adoration. This is how we think, at first, when faced with Zen.

Many people dislike this self-God-like Zen. I am not protected by God, they say. I am a mere man, and there is no God! Zen sneers, some say, at all other religions as superstitions. Zen tries to annihilate all religious feeling—just like Soviet Russia! Other voices are heard saying, "Nothing can help us except science," or "I want something, but with this self-God-like Zen, I can find no God to ask for it. Will not life become dry and worthless?"

I think this feeling is in all civilized people—not merely those who follow the self-God, but all people—agnostics, sophists, or skeptics.

Quite a long time ago, I entered that corner and struggled to make my way out of that limited existence. After a long while, I came to this conclusion: I am making myself limited by my own reason. It is ego or selfhood. Of course, Buddhism emphasizes that we must destroy ego, but *how* to destroy it was my problem! Of course, I studied the sutras and also realized much from meditation. I thought: "Your *I* is not yours; it is an *I* that belongs to the universe; it belongs to all the potential power of the universe. The *I* of the fish, an insect, a cat—all are the same *I*—the *I* of God."

I accepted that. I am not my *I* but the *I* of God, many *I*'s embodied and many *I*'s unembodied—latent *I*'s that sleep like trees, which will develop later to become *I*'s again. Of course, I do not think "I *am*." *I* am not existing.

Thus, through this limited self, I tried to find an avenue to go out and to enlarge. Of course, I must be selfless, non-ego. I thought: I am a body of water that was born in the ocean, in some shape; I broke the utensil and my water united with the water of the ocean—then my self was not so small. My body keeps the seed; my body nourishes the seed; my body bears all seeds, and sees all existences. Well, then, this present physical appearance of Mr. Sasaki is not myself, but the four kings of the four quarters—the god of earth that keeps the seed; the god of water that nourishes the seed; the god of wind, the air that carries sound; the god of light, the fire that shines on things. I have four great gods within me, and I am four great gods. Slowly I realized myself. Now I did not feel I was alone in the universe. The radio apparatus within me began to sing again.

The prayer that I offered to God was not to a god who was severed from or connected with others. To follow my own law, I offered prayer. I decided I must cultivate my wisdom to see outer existence and the human universe. I must cultivate confidence in the outside and thereby keep my own confidence. I must not violate promises I make. I must work very hard and keep my own soul's dignity. If I violate my confidence in ME, I cannot find confidence anywhere.

I remember once when I was a child of about thirteen or fourteen, I was walking a country road alone. I met a boy. He looked at me. He looked about like me. It was a wonderful experience. I felt I was not alone. This was not a self-God existing alone. I made an avenue to escape from that lonesome, squeezed feeling of a self-God, which I described earlier. I returned gradually to the feeling of God as taught by Shinto and Christianity, and I am in the faith of Zen. My helpless feeling was my own error. It should not be so. In Zen, we should also feel the immense nature of God.

NEW YEAR'S

At the beginning of the year, we feel that our life is renewed again. Those who have no religion in their hearts do not feel much significance in this renewal of life. But we feel joy that we have finished the work of the last year and that we shall begin our new work. We feel we must begin our new life from the foundation. It is like doing your housecleaning. You take the carpet up from the floor and dust everything. One who has no true religion does not know this kind of cleaning.

When we have true religion we take refuge in the *dharmakaya*, we have a foundation in the *dharmakaya*. We do not hold any thought, any thing in our minds when we confront the *dharmakaya* and take refuge in it. And we take refuge in this present consciousness. Whether you believe in it or not, it actually exists, so we take refuge, too, in the present moment. We have a religion that gives us a true foundation. Without this, we would not have much meaning in our lives.

I knew an actor—he was my friend. When he became a Buddhist, before he would go on stage, he would recite a mantra. His attitude became entirely different. That is religion. To go to church, kneel down, pray "O God in heaven" is not true religion. In every moment of your life, whatever you do, you must have this bottomless truth. Then you can concentrate on your work, on the moment.

When you eat, why do you cover the table with a cloth and arrange all those different pieces of silver? You do not know it, but it is religion. Religion is in your mind, and with it you are simple and single-minded.

A woodcutter went into the mountains. There he found a baby wolf, took it home, and raised it. The baby wolf followed him like a dog. One day it followed him to the mountain. By mistake, he killed it. As he was cutting down a tree, the baby wolf walked under the tree and it fell on him, crushing him. The woodcutter felt very bad but left the body in the forest and went back home. The wolf's mother found it. Then from the mountain a pack of wolves went down to the village to take revenge on the human beings. The wolves entered the village and ate human babies, horses, and oxen.

A Zen master was consulted about this, and he said, "I will talk to the wolves and stop them from coming down and doing any more harm. One night, he waited by a tree in a clearing the wolves frequented. He meditated there. The wolves came—one, two, three, four. They surrounded him, growling. Suddenly, one leaped over him. When a wolf leaps over your head, the country people say, it shoots urine into your eyes so you cannot see. Then the others moved in to attack him. The Zen master, not moving, unmoved by fear, was meditating, just like a tree, in the consciousness of insentient nature, which never feels fear. The wolves left and did not come again.

Such stories are fictional, but common in Japan and China. It is often told how wolves and tigers surround a monk and fail to frighten him. How does a sage remain calm in such circumstances? He descends to the level of consciousness of insentient nature. These days we cannot do this. We cannot do this because our attention is engaged in an entirely different direction from that of the ancient Zen masters. A Zen master's consciousness is on a level with the consciousness of nature. They did nothing but meditate. Our consciousness is concerned with present civilization.

Our civilization is different from those days. We cannot do what the masters of those days did, and we would not try. We have our own standpoint and would not imitate them. But we must have one thing—the consciousness that is the foundation.

If anyone asked me, "What is religion?" I would say: "My daily life is religion." We do not need to call "O God" or the name of anything. We join hands and concentrate our minds. That is religion.

The Yogachara School of Buddhism is the Buddhism of "Mind only." They thought that all existences are nothing but Mind. Red, yellow, green, blue—that is our mind, not the human mind but natural consciousness. We are parasites upon a greater consciousness. We are parasites upon nature.

The human mind is living in this body. This body is nature. Thoughts are the human being really. If you would like to find the human being in yourself, your thoughts are the human being. Your body is just the body of an animal.

New York City is a structure of mind, an expression of mind. If you go to the country this is just nature, but New York City is nothing but thought. It is very interesting to observe New York City this way. I like the city more than the country because there is more of the human mind about it. The country is nature. City is the nature of human mind, country is the nature of nature's mind. If we withdraw the mind from our so-called psychological system, there is nothing, no red, no blue, and so forth. To the Yogachara school, mind is the only true existence.

In meditation you find another's mind as well as your own when your mind is in the deep training of meditation.

The first part of the training is to annihilate mind; the second is to emancipate mind, to let it go. First stop the mind's movement, then observe its movement. This old Buddhism can be boiled down to that point. After all, there is nothing in Buddhism but to stop your mind movement and to watch it flow. You must practice this every moment.

Then, when you talk with people, when you eat food, you are doing something with your awareness. There is nothing in Buddhism but to find the secret of this natural movement of mind. This is not a philosophy as in the West. The Oriental mystic just meditates. The Westerner thinks it is banality to watch the smallest piece of mind that is in the brain every moment. But when you watch this way for two, three years, you will find your mind is like a beautiful garden, carefully arranged. Watch it night and day. Then, not only will you feel your own mind, but you can find others' minds too. After all the koans have been solved, you learn to observe your own mind and that of others. You learn to guide them and know what is happening in them. All those Zen masters, when there are no koans to study, come into this practice. All the supernatural power to read others' minds comes from this practice.

WE ARE THE MAGI

We don't know what *this* really is, this thing existing here. Sound is created on the eardrum, not in the object, and color is created on the retina of the eye; the object has no color or shape. So what is this which is existing outside? We call it "reality." But what is reality? It is the world that we see in color, in shape, in our own view. The whole world is our own view. We are living in our delusion, so all of us sentient beings are stewing in our own juice. It is called delusion because really there is nothing outside. True objective reality is unknown. The sky is blue, the earth is green. We are the magi. We are the creators of delusion from the basic state of consciousness.

ABANDONMENT

When we are asked by anyone what we are practicing, the answer is: How to give up. First, we give up the world; second, we give up our notions; third, we give up ourselves.

When students have given up "the world," they usually begin to study the sutras and create Buddhist notions. The Zen master must help them abandon all notions and awaken a real attitude. In the third stage, they must give themselves up in order to serve the human world. There are not many Buddhists who reach this stage. If everyone did, there would be no trouble in daily life. I shall illustrate these stages with an allegory.

The bamboo grows from a shoot day by day, until it reaches a height of ten to fifteen feet. Its foliage is deep green and shining. It is beautiful. This first stage is like that of those who have abandoned worldly life and entered the Buddhist life. Their knowledge and philosophy are like the foliage of the bamboo.

In the second stage, to see the bamboo itself, we cut off all the small leaves, all the foliage, and leave only the long, straight bamboo. The cutting is Zen study. In the third stage, the bamboo is cut from its root. What then?

A woman will use the bamboo as a laundry pole to dry her baby's diapers. A boatman will use it to propel his boat. Someone will make a flute out of it, or a basket, or chopsticks.

Many students are glad to be a beautiful bamboo in full leaf, but how many like the idea of being a laundry pole, or a chopstick? To abandon the notion of yourself is very hard, for everyone clings to the ego, to the root. Such a bamboo cannot be used; we can only keep it in the garden.

NO PURPOSE

During a week's vacation in the Catskills, I noticed the trees and the little forest animals. They were putting forth their very best effort in order to live. For them, there is, unconsciously, just one purpose—survival. They are not as highly developed as we are; their state of consciousness is unconsciousness. They strive in an unconscious manner. Why they live is not a problem for them. From their own standpoint, they are not living for any purpose; they are just living. They do not know that they are living; their living is observed by *us*. They do not know that they are ignorant of their own existence, for in them, no intellect exists. They exist as the sky above and the earth beneath them exists. In Buddhism, this state is called "no purpose."

This view shows how very different Buddhism is from Christianity. The Christian believes that existence has a purpose and that the purpose is the realization of some scheme, plan, or idea of God. It is often said that this idea is the consummation of the good, the true, and the beautiful. Furthermore, the Christian believes that everything that exists here on earth is imperfect and that only by realizing God's purpose will we be perfected. When this purpose is realized, all tree leaves will be as the acanthus leaves, without distortion. I suppose there will be no fat men and no skinny ones. Everyone will be as beautiful as a Greek statue. After all, according to the Platonic Idea, the Idea will be realized. To reach the perfection of already existing ends is the goal.

The Buddhist does not take this view. The Buddhist thinks that pushing and squeezing each other, and dividing one's self (all existence) make *one* position. There are fine trees and poor trees, cats and dogs, men and women, long and short, the fat and the thin, the ignorant and the wise; all things emerge from nothingness and take their positions, living their own lives. Sometimes one is larger than another, and at other times one is smaller. This variety in existence is the good, the true and the beautiful. There is no end to this variety; it has always existed for no particular purpose. The only sure thing is that the small will become larger, and then, in the end, will become small again. This is the Buddhist view.

This view is purposelessness. All is purposeless. When the end comes, the Buddhist closes his eyes and dies. We find refuge in this purposelessness. Of course, the Christian finds refuge in his final aim or goal. Usually Christian teachers in the Orient do not like the Buddhist view. They say that it is pessimistic and has no goal. If what the Buddhist believes is true, they say, why should we strive? Having no special goal, the Buddhist attempts to enjoy every day, whether he lives in poverty or in wealth. He does this because he has no purpose or idea to be realized in the future. The Buddhist believes in karma. I was born into a poor family; times were not good. I came to America to spread Buddhism, but America is a Christian country; I could do very little here. If I had some idea of building a temple with a big bell on top and twenty-five Japanese monks inside, and if I worked to bring in three hundred people every time I lectured, there would be no time to speak true Buddhism.

The Buddhist vision of life is very good, and by realizing this in your daily life, you will always be happy.

In Mahayana Buddhism, we do not suppress the desire to live. If I want to go to Europe to study French, I start saving money! In Mahayana we do not suppress such things. Observing all human beings, the Buddha came to the conclusion that human beings must have the means with which to live and that which gives them life. We are not protected by the powers of nature, or nursed like cubs all our lives. We are not in a mother's womb or in nature's womb; we have been born. As the Christian says, we have been driven out of the Garden of Eden; we must live by the sweat of our brow.

The question is: What are we to do to obtain the means with which to live? If we have a method, we must excel in it. If a farmer is to be the best farmer, he must have strong hands. If a cowboy is to be the best cowboy, he has to excel in riding and roping.

In the forest, I observed many occupations—and how many worlds! The chipmunk, for example, lives in secret; it camouflages itself. Its occupation is to hide itself and look like dried leaves. As the snow drops from its branches, the pine tree springs back proudly; it, too, has its occupation. The willow has its drooping branches, swaying in the wind, and in that softness it lives. That is *its* occupation.

What is my occupation? As a religious teacher, I am working to provide you with a place to grow and to die. What kind of religion am I selling? The Christian is selling God in heaven. Others are selling the Pure Land. But it can be like "hanging up a sheep's head and selling dog meat." What am I selling? Nothing!

Bodhidharma came to China and said not a word for nine years. He was selling Great Nothingness. He sold it to China. In these lectures of mine I am selling my Nothingness; it is the greatest thing that can be bought—spaceless and timeless. Can you hear the sound of the hand? Through that sound you will attain the Great Nothingness. I am selling this Great Nothingness, this wonderful Nothingness. I received it from my teacher, after going through many fears, discouragements, and agonies. I am trying to sell you this Nothingness.

PERFECT PEACE OF MIND

If I meet a Buddhist, observe his manner, look into his eyes, and see no peace or tranquillity in him, I know he is not a true Buddhist. For Nirvana, peace, is the ultimate of Buddhism.

There are many meanings in the term Nirvana: extinction, annihilation, sometimes death, but peace is always included. There are six ways to reach Nirvana—the six *paramitas* to carry you from this shore of disturbance to the other shore of peace.

Giving, *dana-paramita,* is one of the ways to reach Nirvana. Buddhists give without purpose, and receive likewise, with no ulterior motive, without knowing whether they are giving or receiving, for they realize that nothing belongs to them. Monks practice this by begging. I am not myself; I am Buddha. You from whom I beg are not yourself; you are Buddha. Therefore, there is no one who gives, and no one who receives.

Observing the precepts, *shila-paramita,* is usually given as the second of the six *paramitas.* If we are quite natural in our attitude, we need no commandments. If you do not smoke or drink, you do not need commandments regarding smoking or drinking. Observing the commandments, you will understand that there is no self. You are a part of Great Nature. The laws of heaven and earth are written in your mind and body. When you realize this, observing the commandments is an easy task; violating them is difficult. There is no one to observe the commandments, and there is no commandment in the whole world! When you reach this conclusion, you are in Nirvana. You have reached it by your wisdom, *prajnaparamita,* the sixth way.

The Buddhist seeks peace, not happiness. Happiness is a cause of agony; to attain happiness, you have to suffer. There is also suffering in the attaining of peace, but it is different. We do not fear it.

We can die in peace. In Japan and China, we offer a drop of water to the dying man, putting it to his lips on the feather of a bird. He cannot see. He cannot hear. In the moment of his death agony, he suffers. But his mind is not dead; he has peace in it. This peace is not easy to attain.

I was in a monastery before I entered the Russo-Japanese War. I spent eight months on the battlefield. I had thought I was a good

Buddhist student; but on that battlefield I realized that something was wrong. I had no peace of mind. My teacher had told me, "If you are a true Buddhist, your mind is always peaceful—even on the cliff of life and death!"

If you understand yourself truly, there will be peace in your mind. You cannot buy it. You may find it in poverty, as well as in riches. Peace is very easy to attain if you really find the way. If you clearly understand where you are in this universe and what you are doing as a person, you can find peace of mind.

Freedom from disturbance is necessary. You must know your own cause of disturbance. You can be disturbed by erroneous instruction, interest in a strange religion, or reading about some "ism" in which you believe and seeing your whole life from that angle. You must observe carefully how your life is altered by such disturbances.

To straighten yourself out, you must meditate and think deeply into your heart and mind. This is *dhyana-paramita*. When you correct your errors, you will see true existence—the true laws of heaven, earth, and man. These three equal religion. Then you will know the law of the country, of the people, of the family, and of the individual. Knowing this, you will have the real view.

The law of man is called morality. The law of heaven is without discrimination: no punishment and no reward, no saint and no criminal—all can be received by those who know how to live in the pure light where all are equal. The law of earth is different: everything is constantly changing. Water becomes steam—fire cannot destroy it, a sword cannot cut it. But when it turns to ice, a saw can cut it and fire can melt it. Each individual has his own laws; each family has its own laws; each country has its own laws. I notice a big difference between the laws of Japan and the United States.

Another cause of disturbance comes from the past. The system of reincarnation is difficult to explain. Today we speak of atavism or inheritance. The human family is really one tree. You lived in the past, and you will be living again in the future. You are an aggregation, not a single element. Mind and body is an organization of elements. Each individual has various elements in his nature. Sometimes one of these elements exhibits itself, sometimes another. The Buddhist counts five or six elements that compose one mental nature. When you talk with someone, striking all the keynotes, you can find the strongest element in his particular nature. We are not simple, single-minded beings; there are inherent elements in us. But there are also parasitic elements imposed upon the true Bodhi tree. It is these that disturb our mind and direct our life. We must find the true nature—our own level—in which we belong.

If you observe your life very carefully, you will find the factors that suggest what you should do. Do not follow blindly; you must find the arrangement of life that is written within you. Then unconscious factors will no longer disturb you. Acquired and erroneous elements can be eliminated fairly easily by close observation; inherent ones are difficult to straighten out. This is the lifelong study of the Buddhist.

Through meditation, your unconscious states, thoughts, and experiences will become evident, and you will gradually come to perfection. This perfection in personality leads to perfection of being. This is the Buddhist ideal; the perfect personality is a buddha. This is, of course, difficult to reach, but through wisdom, *prajnaparamita,* we can conceive perfect truth, perfect virtue, perfect beauty. To conceive this is emancipation by wisdom. One who attains this perfection and realizes this emancipation will attain real Nirvana—perfect peace of mind and body. The endless effort to reach absolute perfection is the main teaching of Buddhism.

WHAT IS A HUMAN BEING?

As a rule of Buddhist practice, the priest of Buddhism bases his sermons upon the sutras. When we speak traditionally about Buddhism, we must prove that our text is written on such a page in such a sutra, and that such a master wrote the commentary in such a way. No Buddhist priest gives his own view of Buddhism. We already have almost six thousand scriptures. For us these are enough. Everything the human mind can think about Buddhism has already been written down. We do not need to add any more. But occasionally, for some reason, a Buddhist priest does give his own view. There is no particular reason at this time, but I shall take this occasion to speak informally.

In his youth the Buddha thought this human world a most obnoxious place; he hated human life and left his home to become a monk. He thought the human being, as a being, was very negligible, but he had no particular idea what to do about it. Following the Hindu conception, he tried to escape from this human consciousness. Finally, he annihilated the concept of the human being and found that there is no such being as that which we call human. According to the Buddhist way of thinking, each human being consists of six different beings: the hell-dweller, the hungry spirit, the beast, the angry spirit, the human, and the heavenly being. From moment to moment this human being appears in different forms: one moment the demon takes its place in the human body, then the god, then death or hell, and finally the body is possessed by the beast. Once in a while the human being appears and possesses this body. Only then is it truly a human being.

Finally the Buddha annihilated everything and found himself worthless. In the sutra it is written that King Mara, the Tempter, appeared before him then and said, "O Tathagata, this is the time for you to enter Nirvana." The Buddha thought, "At any time I can enter Nirvana, but now I must inform my fellow beings why their life is so miserable, why the life of the human being is agony."

This is an aspect of Buddhist teaching on which Hinayana Buddhism places emphasis. Agony, the cause of agony, the annihilation of agony, the way of the annihilation of agony—these are called the Four Noble Truths. This work of annihilation is done by

the Buddha's disciples. The method is meditation. Practicing meditation, finally I annihilated everything I could think of. I annihilated
the outside as an illusion; it is illusory, not real, existence. Then I
annihilated the inside as an illusion: the inside is nothing but shadows of the outside. As the outside is illusory, the inside is also illusory; within and without there is nothing that can be called real.
Not only by thinking but through consciousness, I annihilated
myself. Then what happened? I found my legs! This is the joke. I
had annihilated the universe, and at the end I, the annihilator, was
still sitting there with crossed legs! "At least," I told myself, "I have
found my legs."

Of course, I acknowledge that the world in which we are living
is not exactly as we feel, as we think. But, after all, we must accept
this human life. We must accept—we do not need to call it by
name—this whole thing, inside and outside. The usual human
world is not the real human world; it is a world created by human
hopes and notions. Human beings think of the ideal as truth, good-
ness, and beauty—these three combined make the ideal—and we
think we must reach this. All tree leaves are twisted and unsymmetrical, but each tree leaf wishes it might be symmetrical, even on
both sides, with no warp or irregularity, with no worm eating it.
The chair thinks that the human chair existing now is so imperfect
that it is almost shameful for it to exist in comparison with the chair
existing in the realm of the ideal. The human face, too—it is almost
shameful to carry it around in comparison with the face of Venus. I
went to see the Venus de Milo. Her face is twisted, almost like
mine. I cannot see why it should be thought beautiful. The human
being created this notion of the ideal and tortures himself with it.
We are all imperfect, but that we are inferior is your idea. When I
came to this country I realized what your idea of perfection was
when I saw your gardens: a round fountain in the center with dol-
phins vomiting water at the four corners; white, yellow, and red
flowers in circles; smooth pavements—gardens like mosaics, symmetrical, mathematical. And I thought, "Certainly this is different
from the Oriental idea of beauty."

Everything is irregular in my country. Our idea of beauty is one
stone in water, one pine tree, a bridge, and a lantern. We just cut
off a corner of nature from somewhere and say, "This is beauty!"
Landscape exists for beauty, so we show it. Tree leaves, for
instance, are all unsymmetrical and partly eaten by worms, yet we
think them beautiful, not in the same way as something carved by a

sculptor is beautiful, but they have their own beauty. We don't scold the tree leaves: "I don't want to look at you."

A tea master once asked his disciple to sweep the garden. The disciple watered the garden first, then swept it very clean. It was autumn and the leaves were falling. The disciple swept everything away—all the tree leaves, all the pine needles—and even washed the pebbles. When the tea master came back and saw the garden, he asked, "Have you swept the garden?" "Yes." "You don't know how to sweep a tea garden. Look at it! How can you call yourself a future tea master? Think about it!" What was the disciple to do? He was a wise disciple. He went to the garden and shook the maple tree. Two or three yellow leaves fell down, and some pine needles. "You are a good pupil," said the master. "You understand." This irregularity makes beauty. We expect irregularity and excuse it, even if it is a little too much.

We think of all the world and all human beings in such a way. Our idea of completeness may be likened to the moon reflecting upon the waves. In the sky the moon is perfect, round and full, but in the water it stretches out and comes back, breaks into ten thousand pieces like the scales of a fish—it changes its appearance in a million different ways. But from the synthetic view there is perfection in that irregularity. We understand perfection, but we are not trying to bring it out in our human life. We like to live as human beings, accepting all human qualities; but we must emphasize the beautiful parts and suppress the ugly.

Confucius said, "The superior man cultivates the foundation." "Foundation" means the foundation of the human mind; according to this foundation we perform our daily life. This foundation of the human mind exists between parent and child, brother and sister. It is the foundation of human feeling and human life, and we build human life on that ground. We find it naturally between parent and child, brother and sister. When you open the Confucian *Analects* you find: "A dear friend has come from a distance. It is delightful." This plain feeling is the basic human mind.

There is also an ugly way to associate with others. These days we do not find people of the same calibre as our ancestors. People have become terribly small, and their minds contorted. What is the cause of this? Great men are not found only in fables or legends, we know they existed among the people of ancient days. Why is it we don't find any of that calibre today? Everyone has become so small and so cheap. We must think about this. Everyone knows there is something wrong, somewhere something twisted, but we cannot figure out what it is. In the economic conditions, in the political conditions, something is wrong. We must pass through these conditions. We cannot know what it is or where it comes from, but it is clear that what is wrong comes from the mind. We work so hard, but we don't get anywhere because we are trying to go somewhere on the seat of an automobile. We don't know how to find the real human being. Find your own self, the real human being, the real heart and real mind, the real love that is not distorted, not of ulterior motive. It is pure as spring water. All of us have this, but we have forgotten that we have it and don't know how to find it.

People tell me I am an idiot to think one can be kind all the time. Someone told me, "Everyone laughs at you. You should be hard-boiled." How can I be a hard-boiled egg? "You must be tough," he explained. I went to see a movie about a big newspaper office. In this picture a little boy goes up to a reporter and says, "Chrrk!" with a gesture of cutting his throat, then reads his name from a list of those who are fired. In my father's time, if you discharged an employee, you would speak with him decently; you would call him into your private office and at least say you were sorry. Perhaps the movie was true, perhaps it is done this way nowadays, with no words, no waste of time, just a "Chrrk!" and a fifteen-year job gone. I think no human being likes this. Even the hard-boiled guy in the newspaper office didn't like it. Well, there is something wrong here, isn't there?

I think about the old days, about how my father educated me. After supper he would call me to his chair and educate me. He taught me what it is to be a human being. In the West the mother used to teach the children. These days fathers and mothers put the baby to bed and go out dancing somewhere. The child goes to school, and the schoolteacher gets a salary for dumping out knowledge. No one teaches the child how to develop the qualities of a human being.

I can tell you something of what we were taught in the East. There are five cardinal virtues, the necessary qualities of a human being. Lacking one, you are not complete. The first virtue is love; the second is duty; the third is propriety; the fourth is intelligence; the fifth is confidence.

Love. What is love? We don't need to talk about it. When two human beings meet, naturally there is love: love is felt naturally between two.

Duty. If someone comes and helps you when you are in a predicament, you will remember; if that person is in difficulty, you will help in return. My parents educated me with love, therefore I educate my children in the same way.

Propriety. I always talk about the relationship between parents and children because this is the foundation of propriety. You call your father "Pop." How can you call your father this! If we Japanese were to call our father "Pop," he would be furious. Without propriety, there cannot be warm feelings between husband and wife. And between men there are ways of saying things—you may move the mouth and the lips in the same way, but what a difference!

Intelligence means the sympathetic view. With the sympathetic view you understand the other and forgive him without a word.

Confidence is the fifth of the cardinal virtues. With confidence no one speaks behind another's back; no one gives away a friend or tells secrets. Your friend says, "It is a secret, but I will tell you." But when you know, I know, earth knows, heaven knows. When there is confidence, you listen to your friend, perhaps say just one word, and your friend goes away knowing that he can trust you.

These days the diplomats, who hold the whole power of their countries, come together and talk. One says something one day, but the next day no one can trust what was said yesterday. How can confidence between two countries be established that way?

What are we doing that everyone distrusts the other? These days there are no cardinal virtues in our life. Where shall we seek the true human quality? Without this human quality, on what foundation do you build your life? Any other foundation is like ice that melts away while you are looking at it. Human error is clear. Truth is not outside; it is in you. Of course I am thinking of these Confucian virtues in my Oriental way. You must think of them in your own way. Everyone realizes that something is wrong. I think what is wrong is very clear.

ADAPTABILITY

Day by day, moment by moment, intrinsic adaptability in accordance with circumstances reveals itself.

When you hear the Buddha's teaching, it is the voice of the soul, whispering. You call it "conscience." It does not always work by itself; we may have to dig it out to use it. Sometimes we listen. But it is very hard to take its orders—"Don't eat any more sausage!" But you have already decided—"Just a little more."

It is the sorrow of the human being that we know the "law" but cannot obey it. "Well," some old monk says laughingly, "perhaps that *is* adaptability." I think I agree. After all, adaptability is not always as cold as ice.

When you understand adaptability in accordance with circumstances, you will understand the unity of all existence—the unity between this and that, you and me, the entire world. All is just one soul working by the same law of adaptability. We understand the law of society, of the human being, and of nature, the law of everything. The same law works in the human heart, in the tree, and in the weeds. When I was studying painting, I understood this very clearly. Now it works in Sokei-an, in New York. Giving lectures in this terrible language is the position he must accept. We accept everything.

THE FIVE EYES

The Buddhist term "the five eyes" is quite popular among lay
followers of Buddhism, but they misunderstand its true significance. They think it means some mysterious power that enables
them to see through walls, or hear from a great distance.

The first is the physical eye; the second is the *deva* eye; the third
is the wisdom eye; the fourth is the *dharma* eye; the fifth is the
Buddha eye. The first three eyes are for students; the last two are for
teachers.

The Buddha himself spoke about the *deva* eye many times, and
in the early sutras there are descriptions of the *dharma* eye, but the
term "the five eyes" is used only in the later Mahayana scriptures.
Of course, Buddhist students understand that the technical terms of
Buddhism were not invented by the Buddha himself but were
developed by generations of Buddhist students. In the
Mahaprajnaparamita-sutra (the Great Sutra of Wisdom, not the
short work, but the six-hundred-volume version), I found this line:
"If the Bodhisattva Mahasattva wishes to attain the five eyes, he
must learn *prajna-paramita* through practice." I think this may be
one of the oldest statements about the five eyes that appears in the
Buddhist scriptures. Nagarjuna, in his famous commentary, the
Mahaprajnaparamita-shastra, says:

> With the eye of the flesh (the physical eye), we see what is
> nearby; we cannot see what is far away. We can see the
> front, but we cannot see the back. With that eye, we can
> see the outside, but we cannot see the inside of our mind.
> With that eye, we can see everything in the daytime, but
> we cannot see at night. When we see above, we cannot
> see below. This naked eye is a very inconvenient and
> imperfect eye. Therefore, we agree among ourselves that
> we shall not do anything where no one can see, that we
> will do everything where everyone can see. Therefore, we
> try to attain the *deva* eye. If you attain the *deva* eye, you
> can see near and far, front and back, inside and outside at
> the same time. Day or night, you can see everything. You
> are free to see above and below.

This eye usually belongs to human beings, never to animals.

From the West Side, the sun looks as though it drops down into New Jersey when it sets. The American Indian used to paddle across the Hudson River to reach the place where the sun sank. My ancestors believed that the sun was the size of a tea tray. Civilization has given human beings, generally, the *deva* eye. Now we know how far away the sun is; we know that it doesn't hide in the New Jersey swamps in the evening nor rise from Long Island in the morning. In today's world, the scientific eye is the equivalent of the *deva* eye. With it, we can see the real size of the sun, the real distance to the moon.

This is a fairly good explanation of the *deva* eye, but the true meaning as understood by Buddhists is different. The *deva* eye sees the things that are relative; it sees clearly, but it fails to see the reality of things. It sees in shape and color, time and space. We must attain the eye that is able to see the state of reality of all things, not only the reality of objective existence but the reality of subjective existence.

When you attain the wisdom eye, all differentiated human forms and the forms of nature will disappear from before your eyes, and you will see only one form and one nature, which is Emptiness. Sometimes this is called no-form, no-purpose, no-creation, no-destruction. IT exists from the beginningless beginning to the endless end. No one has created IT, and IT will never be destroyed. IT has no name, no shape, no color. IT is the original state of being. With our physical eye and our *deva* eye, we fail to see the state of reality, but with the wisdom eye we can see IT. The one who has this eye is enlightened. All disciples of the Buddha must attain this.

Using the terminology of Immanuel Kant, this eye might be called "intellectual intuition." According to Kant, there are two kinds of intuition, intellectual and empirical. The state of mind that realizes reality is intellectual intuition in his definition.

Laypeople sometimes misunderstand this. Thinking that the state of reality is some mysterious place, they conceive erroneous ideas about it and delude themselves. Western philosophers and religious teachers have given their own explanations of reality. So please look up "reality" in your own dictionary or encyclopedia, and see what I am talking about.

With the eye that is called the wisdom eye, you can attain Emptiness, but only for yourself. It is not enough to teach others.

With this eye, you cannot promulgate Buddhism to others, though you attain enlightenment for yourself with it. To teach others, you must attain a still higher eye, the *dharma* eye.

When you attain the *dharma* eye, you will see all the different strata of existence. Although you are in the state of Reality, you will not be able to see the many stages and phases in the Dharma until you attain this eye.

There are people who have felt the great cosmic vibration, but cannot transmit it. Many attain great religious insight, but few can teach how to reach it. They require the higher eye, the eye that observes the law of nature—the *dharma* eye. In meditation, we observe the law of mind and analyze mind so as to attain the *dharma* eye. Then we can see the other's state of mind and read it.

When you have entered the endless world of the North Star—the world of the wisdom eye—you must turn yourself from within the North Star to look toward the entire zodiac extending southward. The turning point of enlightenment exists between the wisdom eye and the *dharma* eye. When you enter IT, you must turn yourself around to see where you came from. Then with your enlightened eye, you will see the *entire* nature of the human being. For instance, you will look at a man and see that he can practice one Buddhist way but not another, or that he can enter this avenue but not that one. So, according to the nature of each person, the *bodhisattva* selects the means by which we can practice to attain enlightenment. Those who have this eye understand all law and can switch their own power to another, so that the other can feel it.

But though the *bodhisattva* has attained the *dharma* eye, and understands the Dharma according to Buddhism, his eye does not penetrate the minds of slaves and criminals, of crooked and twisted souls, of the lower sentient beings, or those lost, wandering ones who dwell in hell. The *bodhisattva* can only transmit his power to good and natural followers.

To reach all sentient beings, one must attain the highest eye, the Buddha eye. When the *bodhisattva* attains this eye, it will penetrate everything, even the minds of human beings covered with the beginningless darkness of ignorance and eons of evil karma. The Buddha eye can reach the true heart and the true mind of criminals and slaves, and save them from their agony and give them emancipation. The one who has the Buddha eye sees from all sides; sees all the details of the human mind. With compassion and sympathy, the Buddha eye observes the agony of entanglement and of impurity. Nothing can be hidden. When the Buddha eye sees the washerwoman, cursing and gossiping in the laundry, crying from morning to evening among the soap bubbles and steam, the Buddha eye reaches the truth hidden in her mind and is able to give her emancipation. The Buddha eye penetrates through all the details of the human mind and its emotions. Seeing a man or woman with this eye, the Buddha can clearly see what is wrong with his life, in his nature. The Buddha works for salvation among all kinds of people and sees all there is to see. The one who has this eye sees the concealed psychology of people and saves them. The *bodhisattva* can effect his own salvation with his own wisdom, but the Buddha, with his compassion and sympathy, knowing all human beings' minds and emotions, effects salvation among all of them.

A Zen student asked his teacher, "I have heard that all enlightened teachers go to hell. Why is this?" The teacher said, "If I did not go to hell, how could I save you?"

Ordinary people have attained two eyes: the physical eye and the *deva* eye. Buddhist students who have attained enlightenment have three eyes: the physical eye, the *deva* eye, and the wisdom eye. The *bodhisattva* has four eyes: the physical eye, the *deva* eye, the wisdom eye, and the *dharma* eye. Only Buddha has all five eyes.

To become Buddha, sentient beings must have five eyes. I wish everyone would at least attain the third eye.

THE THREE BODIES OF BUDDHA

There are several fundamental terms in Buddhism. One is very important—"the three bodies of Buddha" (*trikaya*). At the beginning of our meetings, we always say: "I take refuge in Buddha; I take refuge in Dharma; I take refuge in Sangha." These three refuges refer to the three bodies of Buddha. The names of these bodies are *dharmakaya, sambhogakaya,* and *nirmanakaya.* When we observe Buddha as a "person," we observe him in these three ways.

While the Buddha was in the flesh, no one spoke of his three bodies. But after his death, when his disciples could no longer see him, though there were his teachings (the Dharma), and there was his community (the Sangha), there was no Buddha; they had lost the first principle. The Dharma was the Buddha's mind. The Sangha was the Buddha's actions and daily life. But they had lost the master, the soul.

The disciples of the Buddha attempted to find a new master in the Buddha's teachings and the Buddha's community, a master that was not a theory, a doctrine, a fiction, an image, or a personified idea. It must be actually living, must be a reality—as real as what could be seen with their eyes.

Of course, the disciples of the Buddha failed to see Buddha with their physical eyes; they had to find some other eye by which to see Buddha in his invisible state. When with their innermost eye, they saw him in his original state of physical and mental existence, they called this Dharmakaya Buddha.

The Buddha's physical body was scattered to the air long ago. But we can trace back through time, through twenty-five hundred years, to the top of Eagle Mountain near Rajagriha in northern India, and join our palms and worship him as Buddha. This Buddha is still existing. All the Buddha's thoughts and all the Buddha's mind still exist within our mind, and his Reality, his *real* body, *dharmakaya,* is omnipresent. We can find access to the Buddha when we open our *dharma* eye, the eye of Law.

The minds of the disciples of the Buddha are eased when they find the three bodies of Buddha. So, as a true Buddhist, you must know the true meaning of these three bodies.

The three bodies are mentioned by many scholars. Their words have been translated into many languages and commented upon by many scholars, and these terms have appeared in many Buddhist dictionaries. I have glanced through many books since coming to this country, but I have failed to find one that spoke truly about these three bodies.

Dharma is a Sanskrit word with twenty-four meanings. European scholars translate it as "law" or "way" or "religion." I accept the translation of *dharmakaya* as "body of law," but note that in "law" there are three grades.

The first grade is that which we can reach by meditation. It is timeless, spaceless, bodiless. Here, consciousness fails to conceive its own existence. There is no center of consciousness because there is no space or time. The human mind cannot conceive a concept for this first law.

Christians describe IT as outside the universe. They say that the region of "God" is outside the universe and that IT created each of us. Physically, we cannot comprehend "outside the universe," for the universe is endless, spaceless, and infinite. We cannot imagine anything outside space. But we must admit that a state where the power of cognition is annihilated, a state where we cannot cognize the existence of time, space, or motion with our own awareness, our own consciousness, is "outside the universe."

One cannot have faith in this because it is incomprehensible; there is no way to explain it. Of course, philosophically it is explained, but though the philosophers completely explain it, they cannot reveal IT to the mind of man. Immanuel Kant said that Reality is undemonstrable, that there is no way of demonstrating this first law to the human mind. Sages meet there, but, though they know IT, they fail to explain IT. Christian teachers say: "Just have faith. Do not try to reason or argue about IT. IT can be attained only through faith." We Buddhists use a different word—meditation. We say: "Attain IT through meditation."

In meditation, there is no idea, no vision that symbolizes IT. There is just the pure, transparent essence of mind that grasps this existence of absolute law, this *dharmakaya*.

Every religious person, no matter of what faith, must open this door and enter it, must unveil the mystery that is *dharmakaya*. When you think with mind, with words, and when you look for it outside with your five senses, you may find some molecule or atom through your microscope's lens, but you will not find *dharmakaya*.

Words and philosophy lead you to the gate, but words and philosophy, symbols and doctrines, will not send you through the gate. You must enter by yourself, taking off all the vestures that are on your mind.

In ancient days sages, hermits, and ascetics left home and fasted in the desert, not speaking, not using human concepts, and entered immediately. Shakyamuni Buddha attained it under the Bodhi tree and thought at first that he could not speak about it, that it would be better to enter Nirvana immediately. According to legend, the god Brahma appeared and entreated him to stay in the world and promulgate the meaning of *dharmakaya.*

One day the Buddha plucked a lotus, mounted the lion-throne (in the allegory), and held the lotus in his hand. He showed it not with intention but held it casually, as I hold the *hossu* whisk in my hand, and kept himself in silence. Do not misunderstand. There was no throne, and there was no golden-haired lion. There was just a tree stump on which the Buddha sat. He picked a lotus and held it, just as I hold the *hossu,* and kept silent. All the *arhats* looked at him holding the stem of the golden lotus, his eye calm, and could not understand. But Mahakashyapa—the great, the giant Mahakashyapa—understood the Buddha's attitude, and smiled. The Buddha pointed to Mahakashyapa and said: "You have grasped the secret meaning of the highest law. Hereafter, Mahakashyapa, uphold this, and do not lose it. Transmit this to the generations of the future." This was called the first transmission of Zen.

When we attain this practice of *dharmakaya,* we show the hand instead of the lotus.

There is a story of a monk who asked his teacher, "What is the true meaning of *dharma?* And please explain the true meaning of *dharmakaya.*" The teacher said, "If you work all day in the rice field, this evening I shall give you the true answer." So the monk worked hard all day, along with the other monks, thinking that in the evening he would be given a wonderful lecture, that the master would speak in the highest of terms, using words like "omnipotent" and so forth.

Evening came. The monk washed his feet and went to the temple to meet the master with the rest of the monks. The newcomer took his seat, and the master entered (he, too, had been working during the day), went to his place, and sat down. "Now, Master," the new monk said, "please explain to us the true meaning of *dharma."* The master extended his arms with open palms and smiled. That was all. That was the end. Strange? Not at all strange if you see with your innermost eye. You can see it also with your physical eye. The eye must open from the inside.

The second grade is *sambhogakaya,* our own consciousness. A European scholar has translated *sambhogakaya* as "body of enjoyment." Body of enjoyment! Yes, *sambho* is "enjoyment," but this word must be translated as "unity" or "connection" or "yoga." Consciousness cannot exist alone. It must make contact with outer existence.

Really, our own bodies extend to the outside. For instance, a cat playing with its tail forgets that its tail is its own body. We forget in the same way. When we observe the outside "substantiality" as a spiritual existence, then it is the objective experience of subjective mind. The outside is an extension of our consciousness. The outside and consciousness make unity in meditation, that is, yoga with *dharmakaya.* With the physical body and with the active mind, yoga is made with the entire universe, including all the thoughts of the human being. We make yoga with everything to realize our own existing *sambhogakaya.* You can see *dharmakaya* with this *sambhogakaya.* With present consciousness, you can see the inward body and the outward body; you see *dharmakaya* with *sambhogakaya.* You also see *nirmanakaya,* the outward body, the body of transformation. All the many shapes—man, woman, tree, animal, flower—are extensions of the source—*sambhogakaya.*

Thus we complete our conviction that we take refuge in *dharmakaya*; we take refuge in *sambhogakaya*; we take refuge in *nirmanakaya.* Christians say Father, Son, and Holy Spirit. We say Buddha, as an existing body in *dharmakaya.*

The first law, then, is omnipresent. The second law is like light or heat; it has extension and pervades the fourth dimension—all over and at once. The third law is that of *nirmanakaya,* where we cannot go in all directions at once; we have to choose one way, like a one-way street. It does not radiate like a wireless message, but extends in a line like a cable.

We take refuge in the Sangha—group life and the union of sentient life, all sentient life: water, fire, air, earth, and all that we cannot see in a material sense. All that exists in this wonderful sphere is life, nothing but spirit itself.

This is the *trikaya.* Thus we take refuge in Buddha.

BUDDHA'S *DHARMAKAYA*

Buddha's *dharmakaya* has no form. It is not in the ten forms enumerated in the sutra, the so-called forms of sight, sound, smell, taste, and touch, forms of growing, remaining, and decaying, forms of man and woman. How then can it be a body? Buddha's *dharmakaya* is in the state of Nirvana. It is not in the state of this phenomenal world. Buddha was living in this world for a short time, just eighty years, and he was teaching for about forty-nine years. His existence was very short. After Buddha's passing into Nirvana, the Sangha lost the main treasure of its three treasures (Buddha, Dharma, and Sangha). Therefore, the Buddhists had to change their theory. They invented the invisible and unintelligible state of *dharmakaya,* the main state of Buddha, which is existing today. We cannot see Buddha, we cannot hear him, we cannot touch him; he is not growing, remaining, or decaying; he is neither man nor woman. He is in the state of Emptiness. What is Emptiness? How can we prove the existence of Emptiness? It is not something we can see or think about. It is intangible and unintelligible. We cannot know it with our intellect. Then how can it be Buddha? This is the key. This is the great question.

Of course, with human knowledge we cannot think about what is unintelligible. But why do we always have to depend on human knowledge? Why must we always think with words, which we have invented? Is there any way to realize this Emptiness, this existence of Buddha through this Emptiness? We have never seen Emptiness. We cannot think about Emptiness with thoughts. If we think about anything that can be materialized as thoughts, it is not Emptiness; it is something, isn't it? So Buddha's *dharmakaya* is absolutely hidden from human beings. Not only from human beings, but from all sentient beings.

This Emptiness is the object of Buddhism. We have to have faith in it, even though we do not, cannot, understand it. It is very difficult to *think* about Emptiness. When you think about God, you can have faith in God because you believe in God's existence. But Buddha's *dharmakaya,* to us, is non-existence. How can it be God? Therefore, Buddhism is a very strange religion when you think about it.

Buddha's *dharmakaya* has no form. The form of *dharmakaya* is no-form. We have faith in Buddha's *dharmakaya* because it transcends the human mind. We cannot give it a name. We cannot sleep with it like a dream. We cannot talk about it because there is nothing to talk about. When we talk about Buddha's *dharmakaya*, we cannot open our mouths. The ancient Buddhists said it is like a mute trying to talk about a dream. He dreamed something last night, and this morning he wants to talk about it; but he is mute, so he cannot say anything.

No one speaks about the attributes of *dharmakaya* as the Zen priest does, because the priests of other sects hesitate to talk about the *dharmakaya* of Buddha so freely and so plainly. But when I speak about Buddha's second body, *sambhogakaya*, you will find there is some possibility of understanding Buddha's *dharmakaya*, some possibility of realizing it.

When you realize Buddha's second body, you will attain bliss because your eyes and mind will suddenly see Buddha's *dharmakaya*, not with this eye but with the "mysterious eye," which sees the *dharmakaya*. What is the Buddha's second body? It is Buddha's wisdom. Not only Buddha but everyone has this wisdom. Now I am here, and I know that I am here. You are there, and you know that you are there. I breathe in, and I know that I am breathing in. I breathe out, and I know that I am breathing out. I know my inhalation is very slow; I know my exhalation is very slow. Every moment I know my own existence with my respiration, by breathing in and breathing out. This knowing is wisdom, and we realize that we have wisdom. Wisdom is a very primitive power; it is just "to know." Today we use the word wisdom in place of intellect or intelligence, but wisdom is neither intellect nor intelligence. Wisdom is either consciousness or knowing. Temporarily, we divide this into two qualities, one side being the consciousness quality, the other side, intellect. But we do not need to divide it into two. Enlightened wisdom is called *prajna*.

I shall take this opportunity to explain why we practice meditation. We do not practice meditation to digest our food, or to strengthen our stomach muscles or to find the chakras—the centers of energy—in our spine. We practice meditation to find the highest chakra, which is wisdom. We meditate to keep our awareness. This wisdom is called "THIS." It is THIS to me, to you, and to everyone. I do not practice meditation to prove that I have wisdom. It is proven by itself. It is axiomatic. Everyone knows without talking about it. Fire doesn't know that it is shining, but we know it is shining. THIS is the Buddha's second body. Buddha had it, and he has it, and he is continually in it.

Wisdom is not here or there, it is everywhere. The whole universe is wisdom. The whole universe is consciousness. It is here in you, in everyone. When this wisdom is in form, in this body, we see outer existence. When wisdom is in no-form, it is in *dharmakaya*. So when your physical body is destroyed, your wisdom is not destroyed. Your wisdom is there shining, but you have nothing to do with it, nothing to think about it with. You have nothing to look at, but wisdom is there. What wisdom is there? The wisdom that has no physical body, that is called *dharmakaya* wisdom. When *dharmakaya* wisdom is in a physical body, we call it *sambhogakaya*.

Once when I was being operated upon, and I was keeping myself very quiet, I did not feel my body at all. I could hear the sound of instruments and voices. The doctor was directing the nurse; then he came and asked me for my name, address, and so forth. Later, I understood I had not lost consciousness, but that I had lost the medium through which I realized consciousness, through which consciousness functions. The body is its medium. When this body departs, consciousness still exists. Our thoughts are also a medium, a semi-material medium. When we die, this consciousness is scattered. This consciousness is not ours, not yours, not mine, not the consciousness of Mr. Smith, but of Buddha. Not Shakyamuni's nor Mahakashyapa's consciousness, but the consciousness that is universal Buddha. Through *sambhogakaya* directly, immediately, we understand the *dharmakaya* and we know that the *dharmakaya* has no form. We have to practice this without thinking, without talking. We prove it without a word, without thought. It is *sambhogakaya* or *dharmakaya* at this moment. There is no space where we can harbor a doubt.

And now I shall speak about the Buddha's transformation body, *nirmanakaya*. *Nirmanakaya* takes a form—the form of a male, the form of a female. It enters into this form of eye and of ear. It grows, it remains, and it decays. It can be a butcher, a university professor, a monk, a streetwalker, a soldier—anyone. But all are the Buddha's *nirmanakaya*.

It may seem to you that these three bodies are very strange; but think about it. It can be understood plainly. There is no hocus-pocus in it.

There was a monk called Fu Joza who was always giving lectures on the *dharmakaya*. One day he was on the high seat of a famous temple, lecturing as usual on the nature of *dharmakaya*. He was saying that *dharmakaya* exists beyond space, beyond time, that the size of *dharmakaya* is boundless, its life limitless. It exists everywhere, but it has no name. A Zen monk who was listening to the sermon from a seat way back in the audience all of a sudden laughed. What Fu Joza had said seemed very funny to the Zen monk. Fu Joza, hearing this laughter, stopped his sermon, descended from the high seat, came before the Zen monk and said, "I beg your pardon. Is there any error in my speech? If my understanding of the state of *dharmakaya* is erroneous, please teach me." Fu Joza was certainly a very humble monk to ask this in front of an audience of a hundred people. "Very well, Joza," the monk told him. "If you really wish to understand the state of *dharmakaya,* you must give up this teaching and go somewhere and practice meditation for three months. Then you will surely come to *dharmakaya.*"

It is true you cannot see this *dharmakaya,* and you cannot understand it through a lecture. You must prove it, by yourself, through your own meditation.

BUDDHA'S BIRTHDAY

There has always been doubt about the exact date of the Buddha's birth—somehow there is about seven years' difference between our chronology and the records existing in Ceylon. Usually the Buddha's birthday is celebrated in southern Buddhist countries on the full moon in May. But in eastern Buddhist countries, we celebrate his birthday on April 8th of the lunar calendar.

In the sutras the Buddha's mysterious and wonderful story is recorded like mythology. Of course, his first disciples added to the descriptions to honor him, and then later disciples in each generation kept adding more details to the story of his birth, so that over twenty-five hundred years it became a complex mythological story. But behind these elaborated records, we can see some truth.

His father was the rajah of Kapilavastu, a city of the Shakya tribe in northern India. His mother was a queen, Maya by name. The people called her "Mahamaya."

According to the custom of the country, when the birth of the child was approaching, Queen Maya went back to her father's house. (She was the daughter of another Shakya tribe.)

The Shakyas were divided from ancestral times into two parts, one living a little distance from Kapilavastu, about two days' journey away. The castle was built on the far side of the river.

The procession of the Queen slowly approached her father's castle, with many elephants and camels, soldiers, and also many pedestrians, musicians, historians, and court ladies bearing incense pots and musical instruments. At noon, she suddenly fell ill and took refuge from the hot sun in a garden by the roadside, called Lumbini. There was a little pond there; the water was clear and cool, and a seat was spread under a tree. When the time of the Buddha's birth drew near, the tree—like a willow—lowered its branches over the mother and covered her entirely with its shade. She held the branches with her hand, and the Buddha came forth from under her arm.

According to the description, as soon as he was born, the infant Buddha stood and walked seven steps in each of the four directions, then stood in the center and pointed to the sky and the earth and said: "Between heaven and earth, I am the only one to be revered."

One cannot believe that a newborn infant could say such strange words. But later disciples put these lines into the sutras. In accordance with this description in Sanskrit, the Buddha's birth is drawn or carved with the infant standing on a lotus flower and pointing at the sky with the forefinger of his right hand, at the earth with the forefinger of his left hand.

Of course, the Buddha never said these words—do not believe such things—but the idea was conceived by Buddhist monks, and Buddhism has accepted this.

A Buddhist does not try to realize God by repeating prayers or by running to God in the dark, in prayerful concentration, experiencing the ecstasy of reaching God. Nor does he try to reach God by reasoning like a philosopher. The Buddhist avoids both of these attitudes, although in later Buddhism there were many different sects, such as the T'ien-t'ai sect in China, that tried to realize the idea of the Buddha by metaphysical thinking. But the Buddha did not take such an attitude. The original attitude was not that.

The Buddha's Buddhism was, so to speak, simply his realization of God, which in Japanese is called *satori*. He had left his friends, his brothers, and his teachers Ramaputra and Kalama because their attitude was to become one with Brahma in meditation, so that meditation became the main reason for surviving on earth.

The Buddha left them. He could not accept such a theory, and he went alone to sit under the Bodhi tree. All of a sudden—he realized: THIS is God, THIS is ALL! The endless sky is the extension of this body, and the earth, covered with mountains and divided by rivers, is also this very body—and trees and weeds, insects, flowers, animals, and other human beings are also Buddha's body; and this soul is the soul of the universe, the soul of God. He realized that prayer is not necessary to prove God. All of a sudden—"THIS is THAT." THIS is his standpoint. From that day on, the Buddhist takes this attitude: Between heaven and earth, *I* am the only one to be revered. This is the Buddha's standpoint, and it is Buddhism.

In ancient days, and even today, there are three types of attitude toward God. One is that you think God is in heaven, and, kneeling down upon the ground, your head bowed, your brow pressed to the stone, you invoke God in heaven with a sincere and humble spirit. In that moment you think your mind reaches heaven and God listens to you—and your prayer is answered. Then you return to daily life, and you and God are separated. You think you are here and God is in heaven.

Another type of attitude toward God is shown by the one who thinks in metaphysical terms—philosophically. This person is like Rodin's *The Thinker*: he puts everything into words. The tree, the sky, the mountain, and the bird have nothing to do with such a person who can only think thoughts.

We Buddhists do not take either of these attitudes. We are with God every moment, day and night, twenty-four hours—inseparable. Without thinking a word, we grasp the conclusion and never forget. Without using thought or reasoning, when we clasp our hands we know what it is.

So in Buddhism it is the Buddha's body we worship that is the highest. *Dharmakaya* is the highest. We do not call it God. We call it Dharma—the highest. And *I* come next, and all that I do is third. We take refuge in Buddha—IT is Dharma. We take refuge in our self. And we take refuge in Sangha—it is all of us. These are the three refuges of Buddhism. I am the highest, and then deeds.

Between heaven and earth, THIS is the only one to be respected, because THIS is Buddha and Dharma and Sangha. THIS is ME.

Because this is the Buddhist standpoint, you must grasp it firmly. This is our standpoint, and it is true Buddhism. In our open eyes, in our daily mind, we have faith.

SELF-AWAKENING

One day after taking a bath in the stream, the Buddha and his disciples were invited into the house of Ramyaka. Though not a Buddhist, the Brahman Ramyaka often invited the disciples of the Buddha and the Buddha himself to his house. On this occasion he asked the Buddha to relate how he had attained enlightenment and from whom he had received the teaching.

The Buddha said that at first he had followed an ascetic whose name was Arada Kalama. Later he went for instruction to Udraka Ramaputra, who was considered one of the greatest teachers of the time. Ramaputra had received his teaching from his own father, who, in turn, had received it from his father; thus, through many generations, this teaching had been transmitted.

Ramaputra said to the Buddha: "There is no teaching I can give you by speech. You must attain it through meditation. In meditation, you will pass through certain stages. In the end you will reach the highest stage, that of neither thought nor no-thought. In that stage there is no coarse thought, as in the lower stages. In the lower stages, the human mind embraces desire and passion. In the middle stages, from the many impressions which have come from the outside, it creates those notions that are called thoughts. In the highest stage all rough or coarse thoughts are annihilated, but pure thought, pure as crystal, is still there, for without this pure thought the soul would disappear. So this is called the stage where there is neither thought nor no-thought. When you have attained this stage, come back to me."

The Buddha went away and practiced. Later he returned to Ramaputra and demonstrated his attainment—there was no way of speaking about it.

Ramaputra said: "Exactly as you have attained, thus I attained and my father before me. Therefore, you have attained the highest stage."

The Buddha said: "I am not quite satisfied. I think there is a higher stage." And he went away and attained the highest stage, the stage no one had attained before him.

After his enlightenment, the Buddha stayed under the Bodhi tree for about three weeks, then went to Varanasi. On the way he met Upaka. In a sutra, this encounter is noted as told by the Buddha:

> At that time the heretic Upaka saw me approaching and accosted me thus: "O Gotama, O Wise One, your expression is pure, your appearance is beautiful, and your face is luminous! O Gotama, O Wise One, who is your teacher? Whose teaching do you follow, and what *dharma* do you make your faith?" Then, for Upaka's sake, I made a verse in answer:

> > I am the highest, I am the mightiest.
> >
> > To no *dharma*, whatsoever, am I attached.
> >
> > From all cravings am I released.
> >
> > Self-awakening only I call my teacher.
> >
> > None other is so mighty;
> >
> > None so peerless.
> >
> > Self-awakening is the highest awakening.

When I was a young novice, I thought, "Why does the Buddha, who has so marvelous a personality, speak in such a loud voice?" I asked this question of a monk. He said, "Because you are a small person, you think in this way. When *you* call yourself a wise man, you think you are superior. So when the Buddha says, 'I am the highest, I am the mightiest,' you think him very haughty, very arrogant. But this is merely from your standpoint. The Buddha attained the highest enlightenment, so to him, he and everyone else are one and the same. He doesn't think 'he' or 'you' or 'I'; he thinks there is only one person in the world, not two. It was from that standpoint that he said, 'I am the highest, I am the mightiest.' He makes us high also. You must observe him not from your small standpoint but from his standpoint."

"I am the mightiest!" In my old age I read this part and find nothing strange. My father used to say: "When you give advice, include yourself in your advice, then your advice will not offend. When there is no difference between yourself and your friend, he cannot take offense." These words come to mind when I think of this passage.

"To no *dharma*, whatsoever, am I attached." Buddha's Dharma is the only one that exists beyond speech. Dharma here is teaching.

"From all cravings am I released." I do not cling to any notions whatsoever. I am emancipated from all self-made notions.

"Self-awakening only I call my teacher." "Self-awakening" is awakening to one's own self. But this self is a Great Self. Not this self called Mr. Smith, but the Self that has no name, which is everywhere. Everyone can be this Self that is the Great Self, but you cannot awaken to this Self through your own notions. When you abandon your self—your notions, your thoughts, your desires—all of a sudden you will find your Self there. You do not need to go anywhere. You find you are already there.

"None other is so mighty; none so peerless. Self-awakening is the highest awakening." We emphasize *Self*-awakening here. The Buddha called his awakening that which he "had attained without teaching."

The records show that the Buddha had both Arada Kalama and Udraka Ramaputra as his teachers, and that from them he learned meditation, so it cannot be said that he had no teachers. But when the Buddha attained awakening, he did so by himself.

In the real sense, no awakened Buddhist has had a teacher. I cannot bring you to awakening. You must do it yourself. The Buddha said: "There is no teacher. Self-awakening is the highest teacher." Please remember this.

THE BUDDHA'S ATTITUDE

In the *Dighanikaya Sutra* is one of the oldest descriptions of Buddhism, the famous account of the Buddha's attitude—his own faith.

The Buddha, in his last days, being about eighty years of age, was approaching Kusinara, where he was to enter Nirvana. In that stricken land, he could not keep his 1,250 disciples around him, so he ordered them to scatter and support themselves. He was in a hurry to reach the Sala tree grove in Kusinara with Ananda, his personal attendant.

Ananda asked the Buddha, "Tathagata, your Nirvana is approaching. Why don't you gather all the disciples once more to deliver your last sermon?"

The Buddha answered: "I have told them all my thoughts, and I have told them all the stages that I have passed through. But if they have no experience in themselves, they are deaf to my words. I have enlightenment, and I have succeeded. They must do likewise. I do not speak to them of my experience to keep them always with me, or to gather them for my benefit. I have told them once of my experience, and once is enough. Why gather them and take away the time they need to practice to attain their own experience? The words that they could understand I have already spoken—why repeat it once more?"

If you have your own experience, and another tells you about his experience, you will understand immediately. But if you have no experience yourself, though someone speaks from the mountaintop, you will not understand.

In Buddhism, students exert themselves to open their minds and to settle their own questions about life, nature, and the universe. There is not much time to speak to others.

It is said that Buddhists take a selfish attitude, trying to make something for *themselves*—that they are unaware of the struggle of others. They are inactive, these Buddhist monks, always living in the mountains or the woods, and having little relation to the outside.

Today, the monks in Japan try to imitate Christianity by teaching the children in Sunday school. But some schools of Buddhism in Japan still keep the old style—no active work on the outside.

My sect, Zen, is a very inactive one. We are busy with our own study to enlighten ourselves first, and then if there is some time left in life, we help others as a repayment of the favor of Shakyamuni Buddha. Our attitude toward teaching Buddhism is to repay the favor of having received the "milk of *dharma*"—to repay the teacher's favor. The baby is weaned, and accepts the milk of the law from the teacher. We nourish ourselves and open our eye to see the true law of the universe, nature, and man. When we come to this place, we do not puzzle, we do not doubt life as we are living it. We are emancipated. Somehow the outside is not dark, and the inside is clear. We thank our teacher and we thank the original teacher, Shakyamuni Buddha. But we must do something to repay that favor, so we teach others as repayment—not for any ulterior motive, such as money or fame—we just repay what we can. If we find no opportunity, then we wait until the time comes; if we have no audience, we just wait. So if anyone comes to me, I will seize the opportunity to repay the Buddha's favor.

We hope to keep this teaching a long time—through human life and into the future—but we cannot create another's enlightenment. I cannot eat your food for you. You must put on your own vesture—I cannot put it on for you. Sometimes we are in doubt as to what to do, how to teach, how to gather pupils—but all such thought is really unnecessary. I think and I work, and if I have more time, then I repay more. If I have no opportunity, I shall wait. This must be the attitude of the religious teacher and of the religious student. It is not necessary to do any other work. The teacher's own enlightenment need not be advertised; there should be no criticism of place or people. We just hold to clarity of mind. If the teacher has true faith and can give the understanding of true religion, that is all—you will come.

PRATYAYA

The understanding of reciprocal relations is quite an old thing in Asia. Everything exists in interdependence with something else. Today you use the word "relativity," but even that is a new word.

We think about length, but we cannot think of length without thinking of width and depth. When thinking about this present moment, we must think of past and future. What is the ceiling without the floor and pillars that support it? How can we speak of a hand except in relation to the other parts of the body? Thinking of myself, I think of my parents, uncles, aunts, friends—all my "relations."

Your friend becomes famous as an artist. You think, "My friend was with me in school and he was rather stupid, but now he is famous. If he hadn't been in this particular environment, he would never have become a famous artist. He's just the type for today, and that's why he was able to become famous." Here is a futuristic painter who has become very famous because these modern times support him. But there were no such thoughts in the nineteenth century. In China and Japan you will find wood carvings not even completed—just one line or tracing or square in a corner somewhere. In their time they were not appreciated, but today they are museum pieces. We call them the first cubist art, the first futurist art.

Who defeated Napoleon at Moscow? Did the Russians do it alone? Or was it that bitter cold winter? Perhaps if it had been summer, Napoleon would have given us a different story for our history books.

In the Orient if a man becomes famous, he cannot take credit for his success. It is the time and place! I sowed some sunflower seeds in my window box; some of them shriveled and died and some grew tall and very strong. I did not *intend* it, but accidentally or fortunately, the lucky ones fell into good circumstances and found their opportunities.

Those who are born without a good environment have no reason to be depressed. Even though a man was born in a cellar somewhere in a dark suburb or slum, with no family or friends to pick him up and place him somewhere, if he has his own strong willpower, he will find some opportunity to express himself. Maybe he will become a famous racketeer or find himself in a good job.

I came here, and I am preaching Buddhism. I did not intend it, but my teacher brought me to America when I was young. I studied my ABC's and went back to Japan, planning to remain there. But somehow that Columbia River and that range of the Rocky Mountains stuck in my dreams. Then I was asked to return here, and I came. Sometimes I am pulled to Japan, sometimes to America, like a rubber ball. This is also a reciprocal relation.

AN AFTERWORD:
LOOKING BACK AT FIFTY-FIVE

When I started to study Buddhism and was studying koans, Zen and Buddhism seemed from my height to be the size of the whole universe. Today, I must confess Buddhism and Zen are just some old furniture in the corner of my mind. I, today, a man at the age of fifty-five, really enjoy my own mind more than Zen and Buddhism. But this was a gift from Buddhism, so I appreciate the kindness of Buddhism. This, our heart, is important. We must have something that is original, that is not Buddhism or Zen, that is science, religion, or philosophy. I did not find it for a long, long time—and Buddhism and Zen were a hard burden. Now I speak about Buddhism and Zen in lectures; but when I am alone I do not speak or think about Buddhism. I enjoy something that has no name but that is quite natural. Perhaps you call it the Pure Land. It is wonderful, the Pure Land. Someone asked me to go for a vacation to Nyack for one month, but I refused. I just stay here and live in my own pure mind.

APPENDIX

HOW IT WAS AT SOKEI-AN'S

The Zen talks given by Sokei-an from 1930 to 1944 were of several types. Some began with a translation of a text and continued with Sokei-an's commentary on it. Others consisted of explanations and illustrations of Buddhist terms. Most striking were Sokei-an's statements of his own thoughts. As it was on first hearing Sokei-an's talks that I was brought to Zen, I naturally regard this collection as a potent factor in carrying on his teaching.

I can recall my first experiences at Sokei-an's vividly. The room in which Sokei-an lived and taught in the thirties was not large. One entered at a door near the front, where his reading desk stood, and confronted the audience before taking a seat. Edna Kenton, a writer, was the organization's historian when I arrived in 1938. She told me later that I had seemed to regard everyone suspiciously, as though I wondered what kind of people might be gathered to hear a Japanese priest. The secretary, Helen Scott Townsend, announced that Shramana[1] Sokei-an Sasaki, Abbot of Jofuku-in,[2] would speak.

The meeting began with the members of the audience sitting in meditation in chairs. During this time Sokei-an, whom we were told to call Osho,[3] sat with us. It was, of course, his SILENCE that brought us into IT with him. It was as if, by creating a vacuum, he drew all into the One after him. It was not a long meditation, at most half an hour. What followed was not a break from it, but a continuation or continuum, during which those who were *sanzen* students "entered the Teacher's room," a small space closed off from the audience by a pair of folding doors on which Sokei-an had pasted the pages of a sutra. The interview between master and disciple behind those doors was the means by which Sokei-an brought his students to the practice of Zen. Whereas in Japan stu-

[1] Shramana is a Sanskrit term for a Buddhist monk or ascetic.

[2] Jofuku-in, in Hakone, in present-day Kanagawa prefecture, is a branch temple of Daitoku-ji in Kyoto. Sokei-an was ordained a priest of this temple and made abbot in 1935.

[3] Osho is a Japanese term of address for a Buddhist priest or abbot.

dents would have begun with long sessions of cross-legged sitting, here the majority of the members were mature people whose sedentary lives did not include physical training. Some did practice meditation in the cross-legged posture at home. Behind those doors, so far as I know, there were no psychological or philosophical discussions, no worldly advice or explanations—just the business of Zen. When in recent years I was asked if we were given "instruction" in Zen, my considered answer had to be "no." To those of us who received Sokei-an's teaching, the word "instruction" is a misnomer. His way of transmitting the Dharma was on a completely different level. One could say he "demonstrated" SILENCE, but it would still give no indication of how he "got it across" or awakened it or transmitted it.

The *sanzen* students would stay inside differing lengths of time, the periods punctuated by the *sanzen* bell, which meant dismissal. Although what was said was usually in too low a voice to be heard outside, there would occasionally be diversions. Shouts or roars would replace the murmurs or silences from within. When the last person had gone in and come out—usually me, in later years—the gong or wooden fish drum would signal that *sanzen* had come to an end. Once, when I had not taken my turn because of some mental disturbance, an awesome shout addressed to me from within reminded me that the Zen student cannot permit worldly matters to interfere with study. As each student came out, his or her face would reveal something of what had transpired. Determination, wounded pride, studied indifference—what a variety of possible responses there were! Of course, we weren't supposed to look at them.

Then Sokei-an would issue from his lair and take a seat at the table on which his manuscript rested on its wooden stand. At one side was the crystal glass, often referred to in his talks, which was refilled as needed from a metal pot that kept his drinking water fairly cool. How hot it was in the little room on summer nights! How many times Sokei-an's carefully folded white linen handkerchief would be needed! Perspiration would drip from our brows, and drowsiness would lower our eyelids, as the fan lulled us with its hypnotic drone. A small gong marked the beginning and end of the service. Before beginning the talk itself, the ceremonial fly whisk called a *hossu* was always raised. When we saw Sokei-an raise the *hossu*, we were not concerned with its symbology. It was just the thing itself. Everything was quite clear. Then the deep voice would begin. As is common with Japanese speakers, some sort of sound, midway between a purr and a growl, would come from the very depths of his being before the first word was articulated. The rest followed naturally.

Sokei-an spoke extremely slowly, and would pause between phrases or sentences for what sometimes seemed an eternity. His accent was a hindrance to some; to others it was an added attraction. (In one of the first talks I heard, I was unsure whether something was being "unleveled" or "unraveled.") After the text, Sokei-an did no more reading. All was given spontaneously. The same subject might be treated many times, but each time the details would vary, as Sokei-an's mind chewed the subject slowly in order to get from it every bit of nourishment possible.

When Sokei-an would come to a story, his dramatic side would take over. All the roles would be played rather than told. Even Stanislavsky might have taken a lesson here. For Sokei-an played not only the human roles, but also the animal, mineral, and vegetable. Sometimes he would be a huge golden mountain, sometimes a lonely coyote on the plains; at other times a willowy Chinese princess or Japanese geisha would appear before our eyes. Best of all were the Zen stories in which he would be the arrogant samurai, the uneasy monk, the frightening ghost, and the stern or kindly master. There was something of Kabuki's technique, and something of Noh's otherworldliness, something of a fairy story for children, and something of ancient Japan. Yet it was as universal as a baby's first "Waaah!" All in all, it was himself he revealed to us, an enlightened human being.

Mary Farkas

The "weathermark" identifies this book as a production of Weatherhill, Inc., publishers of fine books on Asia and the Pacific. Editorial supervision: Meg Taylor. Book design and typography: Liz Trovato. Production supervision: Bill Rose. Text composition: G & H SOHO, Inc., Hoboken, New Jersey. Printing and binding: Arcata Graphics, Fairfield, Pennsylvania. The typeface used in the text is Optima; display type is Copperplate.

call father ↘
su about alz drug @ Pfizer
add Anne for Atlanta referral